ENCOUNTERS
WITH THE
HOLY SPIRIT

JOHN PIIPPO
AND
JANICE TRIGG

WESTBOW
P R E S S®
A DIVISION OF THOMAS NELSON
& ZONDERVAN

WestBow Press books may be ordered through booksellers or by contacting:

WestBow Press
A Division of Thomas Nelson & Zondervan
1663 Liberty Drive
Bloomington, IN 47403
www.westbowpress.com
1 (866) 928-1240

Cover art by Nicole Griffith.
Colossians323arts@gmail.com

ISBN: 978-1-9736-6398-0 (sc)
ISBN: 978-1-9736-6400-0 (hc)
ISBN: 978-1-9736-6399-7 (e)

Library of Congress Control Number: 2019906641

Print information available on the last page.

WestBow Press rev. date: 6/11/2019

Dedicated, with thanksgiving and love,
to the men and women who founded the American
Baptist Charismatic Fellowship,
now known as Holy Spirit Renewal Ministries.
Special thanks to Ken Pagaard, Joe Atkinson, and Gary Clark
for their key leadership in the early years.
We stand on their shoulders in our current efforts
to empower Christians and churches
to fulfill their destiny in Christ.

CONTENTS

INTRODUCTION
JOHN PIIPPO

This book is about how the Holy Spirit turned a conference into a family.

My wife Linda and I became part of this family in 1992. We attend and speak at many conferences, most of which are excellent. But this one has become our favorite. It is a lifeline, having a distinctive deposit, of which we are recipients and transmitters. Much of what we know about the Holy Spirit has been imparted to us at the annual Holy Spirit Renewal Ministries (HSRM) Conference held at the Green Lake Conference Center in Green Lake, Wisconsin.

From 1981 to 1992 Linda and I were campus pastors at the Baptist Student Center at Michigan State University. Those were great years for us. We loved the students and faculty who were part of our ministry. They were from all over the United States. And, we had many international students. What a learning and growing experience this was! Lifelong friendships were formed.

Around 1990 we discerned that God was going to take us away from campus ministry and into a church. One hard thing about campus ministry was investing in and developing student leaders, only to see all of them graduate and leave. We desired to be pastors in a more consistent Jesus-community. So, in 1992, God called us to serve at Redeemer Fellowship Church in Monroe, Michigan. We are in our twenty-seventh year with our beautiful Redeemer family!

Redeemer was part of the charismatic movement in America. This movement extended into our denomination, American Baptist Churches USA. We are a Baptist-evangelical church, pentecostally affirming that all of the spiritual gifts are for today. Redeemer is what I call a Presence-Driven Church (see my book *Leading the Presence-Driven Church*). We have found this way of being a church attractive, and are grateful to be part of it.

Redeemer has been part of HSRM since the latter's inception. So, when we arrived in Monroe, Linda and I were expected to attend the summer conference. We did. We were not disappointed. This was exactly what we needed at the time. For the past twenty-seven years HSRM events have been a vital part of our spiritual lives.

The main speaker at the 1992 conference was Jack Hayford. Jack was one of my spiritual and pastoral heroes. I read his books, saw him on TV, and listened to his sermons. He spoke at two Promise Keepers events, and I was there. Jack wrote the enduring worship song "Majesty." I saw him as a great pastor and leader. I was being mentored by him, even though I had never met him.

Have you ever been to a conference, or a worship event, where a line in a song, or a sentence in a sermon, was highlighted for you? As Jack spoke and ministered to people it seemed that the Holy Spirit had orchestrated things just for me and Linda.

One of Jack's messages was on overcoming fear. I have never forgotten when he said, "fear is a lie." On that summer day in June 1992 the Holy Spirit carved those words on the walls of my heart. In retrospect, the beauty and power of that day brought healing and deliverance. I felt lighter, freer, less burdened, than when I arrived at the conference.

This was a new beginning for us. We were being met and ministered to by the Holy Spirit, who is God's empowering, personal presence! (See Gordon Fee's monumental book on the Holy Spirit in Paul's Letters, *God's Empowering Presence*. See also the biblical book of *Acts*.)

I am an academic. I earned a PhD in Philosophical Theology from Northwestern University. I recently retired from eighteen years of teaching Logic, Western Philosophy, and Philosophy of Religion at our county community college. I have taught at various theological seminaries, including the doctoral programs at Palmer Theological Seminary and Northern Baptist Theological Seminary. I love studying. I value clear thinking. This is important, because experience and feeling without logic can lead to heresy. But this, also, is important: clarity of thought and reason without experience and encounter is empty.

The purpose of Scripture is not to know Scripture. It is to know God, and be known by God. Inexorably, this involves feeling and emotion. This is how God has made us. And this has been part of HSRM's great appeal to us. Like two wings of an airplane, we need the academic and the experiential. HSRM provides that for us. This can be seen in the theological variety of speakers we have had, to include Hayford, Gordon Fee, Clark Pinnock, Francis and Judith McNutt, Charles Kraft, Bill Johnson, J. P. Moreland, Randy Clark, Greg Boyd, Wendy and Steve Backlund, and Michael Brown.

In this book you will meet many of my HSRM sisters and brothers. They share things they have learned about the Holy Spirit, intellectually and experientially. These form core beliefs about the Spirit, which we are pleased to present to you. They include:

The Holy Spirit takes us further and deeper into God's kingdom realities. The Holy Spirit invites us to more growth in Christ. In *The Chronicles of Narnia* C. S. Lewis describes heaven as a place where our experience is "further up, further in." The Holy Spirit prepares us for eternity by taking us further up and further into God's beautiful kingdom, in our pre-heavenly existence.

The Holy Spirit moves prophetically. When the Holy Spirit manifests among us it is not only for our present experience. It can be a preparation for something the Spirit will have for us in the future. In this way the Holy Spirit trains and equips us for ministry in the days ahead.

The Holy Spirit speaks through other believers to strengthen, comfort, and encourage us. That's what, in the early church in the book of Acts, the variety of Spirit-manifestations were for. How good it is to be part of a Jesus-fellowship where this happens.

The Holy Spirit produces staying power. The presence of God's Spirit equips us to host his presence every day.

The Holy Spirit comes with healing power. Most of what I know about praying for healing has been acquired through HSRM.

The Holy Spirit builds family. The Spirit creates meaningful, life-giving togetherness. This is why I call our summer events "more than a conference, it's a family!"

The Holy Spirit desires to conference with the greater body of Christ, and calls us to meet together. For example, one of our speakers was the leader of the Roman Catholic Charismatic Renewal of Wisconsin.

The Holy Spirit is fully available to children. HSRM teaches the same material to kids who attend the conference, with age-appropriate presentations.

The Holy Spirit assures us that we are sons and daughters of God. In a world where people are struggling to find their identities, even resorting to identity-creation on social media, the Holy Spirit seals us with who we are, in Christ.

The Holy Spirit produces boldness in us.

And, as my HSRM colleague Dr. Clay Ford writes, the Holy Spirit…
… gives us life.
…illuminates our intellects.
…sanctifies our emotions.
…refines our character.
…instills godly values and reverence for God's Word.
…motivates our wills and empowers our witness.

…moves our hearts.

…enables a relationship of love and trust with God.

…enables us to perceive the spiritual dimension of life and to navigate effectively in it.

…makes God's presence real to us and inspires our worship of him.

…fills us with love and makes us a family.

As I am writing this another HSRM summer conference is approaching. It will be five days together, reuniting as a family, with new believers joining us, in pursuit of our God, desiring to know and experience more of the Holy Spirit. I am certain there are many other Christian venues that do the same. In these days we need them all!

We desperately need, in our country and around the world, more of the Holy Spirit's manifest presence in love, truth, and power. Linda and I have found a fellowship that believes the same.

Thanks to all my friends who have contributed to this book.

Thank you to Janice Trigg for co-editing this book with me.

Thank you to the many HSRM people who have become, over the years, family to us.

Blessings,
Dr. John Piippo
National Co-Director, HSRM
Hsrm.org

1

THE HOLY SPIRIT AND LOVE
ANNIE DIESELBERG

My first introduction to Holy Spirit Renewal Ministries (HSRM) was when Pastor Clay Ford invited me to speak at the HSRM Conference in 2008. I was intrigued when he told me it was a conference which welcomed the movement of the Holy Spirit. I received the baptism of the Holy Spirit at eighteen, but as a Baptist I was not often in an environment where the gifts of the Spirit were openly practiced.

I have been to many conferences. I enjoy most of them, make good connections, and am often inspired by great teachings. In 2008 I was hungry for more. When I attended the HSRM Conference, I immediately noticed something different about this conference, something that captured me, and has kept me coming back year after year.

I noticed the difference in the wonderful Spirit-filled worship, and the tangible presence of the Holy Spirit. I loved being able to worship in the Spirit freely, without feeling like I was the only one raising my hands or speaking in tongues. As I looked around the room, I saw people expressing their worship to God in a variety of ways. There was no right or wrong way. Everyone was caught up in the Spirit in their own unique way of worshiping God. It was a beautiful thing to experience.

I was excited when I heard one of the conference speakers begin to share prophetic words with the attendees. At the end of every night's service there was an invitation to come forward for prayer. There was a rush of people, desperate for more of God. I was moved by the love of God expressed tangibly through prayers for healing and deliverance, in prophetic words, and with counseling. This open demonstration of the gifts of the Spirit was refreshing, renewing, and exciting. I felt I had found my people group! I was excited to learn more about HSRM.

As one of the main speakers at the HSRM Conference in 2008, I shared stories of my work through NightLight ministry with prostituted women in Thailand. The stories are sometimes heartbreaking. But through this ministry I, too, have experienced God's heart for the broken.

As I shared my passion for sharing God's love to those on the margins, the response was encouraging. Towards the end of the conference, I was approached and told that the executive committee of HSRM, backed by a generous donor, wanted to help us purchase a building to increase the capacity of the ministry. I was overwhelmed! What I had shared had been taken to heart. Here was a group that was responding with more than just words of praise and encouragement.

These brothers and sisters wanted to tangibly express the love of God in a big step of faith, and a commitment to take action. This was a clear sign to me that this was a movement - a ministry that was bigger than a conference event. These were believers for whom being filled with the Holy Spirit produced fruit. I thought I was coming to speak at a conference. But instead of a speaking engagement, I found a family of believers who not only operated in the gifts of the Spirit, but generously demonstrated love as one of the fruit of the Spirit. This authentic love that takes action near and far is a core distinctive of HSRM.

In my travels around the world I have become aware of a desperate hunger for more of the Holy Spirit's manifestations among the people of God. Thailand is a Buddhist and animistic country where less than two percent of the population is Christian. When there are meetings with well-known speakers bringing prophecies, words of knowledge, and gifts of healing, the room is packed. It is amazing to be part of these gatherings, and to watch people being blessed through worship, holy laughter, prophetic words, and healings. It is comforting and reassuring to be in a room filled with believers, soaking in the presence of the Holy Spirit, in a country with so few Christians.

After attending a few of these meetings in Bangkok, I noticed that the same people were coming each time and rushing to the front for an impartation. We smiled at each other and said, "God bless you," and that was about it. I felt no connection to the people attending, though I had seen them many times. I sensed that, for many, this was their spiritual spa. It was a time of soaking, refreshing, excitement, and being reminded of God's power and love. People were drawn from around this spiritually dark city to soak in the Light, be refilled, and depart with renewed lives.

I also treated it like a spa, and came for my own refilling. But I started to become dissatisfied with this. I wanted more. The red-light area was just minutes away, and I wanted to see the power of the Holy Spirit confront the darkness. I wanted to see people filled with the Spirit, compelled by love, reaching out and ministering to those in bondage to the darkness. I wanted to see the fruit of the Spirit's full expression in love. I needed the filling of the Holy Spirit to empower me to bear fruit and fulfill the command of Jesus to love my neighbors as I love myself.

First Corinthians 13 is probably the most quoted chapter in the Bible on love. Aside from describing the characteristics of love, it is also a wake-up call for a generation running after demonstrations of the gifts, but not producing the fruit of love. We read:

> *If I speak in the tongues of men or of angels,*
> *but do not have love,*
> *I am only a resounding gong or a clanging cymbal.*
> *If I have the gift of prophecy*

> *and can fathom all mysteries*
> *and all knowledge,*
> *and if I have a faith that can move mountains,*
> *but do not have love,*
> *I am nothing."*
> I Corinthians 13:1-2

Unless I have love, I am nothing. This foundational truth determines the impact and longevity of every Christian ministry, including those in the Charismatic movement. If the goal is to follow and/or operate in signs and wonders, but love is not the compelling force, then it will come to nothing.

HSRM has had its share of spa-seekers. When popular speakers known to operate in gifts of the Spirit are scheduled at the annual conference, new people register and come early to save seats at the front, hoping they will be called out for a prophetic word or an impartation. The people who flock to hear these speakers are not the ones who show up for early morning worship, the workshops, the boat rides, the sharing of meals, long engaging conversations, or the late-night family gatherings.

We rarely get to know people who come and go. All are welcomed, and the long-termers reach out to them in love regardless of their reason for attending. God is faithful to bless them as well. But, sadly, when they come and go, they miss out on the greater and more powerful undercurrent of love that outlasts the speakers and the conference.

HSRM is much more than a conference with great anointed speakers. It is more than a spiritual spa. It is more than an impartation of blessing and gifts. It is a beautiful family of love. This growing family comes back year after year, regardless of the fame or media presence of the people speaking. They come eager and prepared to hear God's voice, and to serve one another in love. The love of God expressed through this Jesus-community is what keeps us connected and keeps us coming back time and time again. This kind of ministry is powerful and lasting. The Holy Spirit is evident through this community by its fruit. Of this fruit, the greatest is love.

HSRM is a beautiful and unique family, with open arms to people of many Christian denominations. Our common foundation is Jesus as Lord, the Word of God, an openness to the gifts of the Spirit of God, and a deep hunger to grow in the knowledge of God with each other. There is a commitment to a bond of love that grows and overflows without limits.

In Galatians 5:22-23 *The Passion Translation* expresses this core distinctive beautifully:

> "*But the fruit produced by the Holy Spirit within you*
> *is divine love in all its varied expressions:*
> *joy that overflows,*
> *peace that subdues,*
> *patience that endures,*
> *kindness in action,*
> *a life full of virtue,*
> *faith that prevails,*
> *gentleness of heart,*
> *and strength of spirit.*
> *Never set the law above these qualities*
> *for they are meant to be limitless.*"

Through HSRM, love is expressed in many ways. At our conferences, *joy overflows*. Worshipers are comfortable jumping, waving flags in worship, dancing, laughing, or standing serenely basking in the joy, hands at their sides. The atmosphere is contagious! Love is there, with people freely expressing themselves without being judged or restrained.

Churches and families of HSRM reach out to teenagers and young adults who come from broken homes, or struggle with difficult situations. Through the HSRM community *peace subdues* the demons that torment these afflicted ones, and they begin to find their healing.

Patience endures with those who run against the tide, stand out awkwardly with their unique expression of their pain, or are desperate for belonging.

Kindness is seen in action as love is demonstrated across age groups. Singles and the lonely are brought into family groups and given a place to belong. Practical and physical needs are shared, and often addressed. Those who suffer in health are prayed for, and often receive healing. The people who have been in the movement for years set an example of *a life full of virtue*, and are happy to mentor and teach those who are still finding their way.

Faith prevails and *strength of spirit* increases through testimony after testimony of God's goodness.

Gentleness of heart is evident in the welcome, the hugs, the conversations, and the inclusiveness of the ones who hesitate on the sidelines. Prayer counselors keep an eye out for the silent weeper. Their gentleness is evident as they offer prayers and words of encouragement.

The fruit of the Spirit – *love* - is a core distinctive of HSRM. This divine love is expressed in varied ways. It is this authentic demonstration of God's love which ultimately brings people back time and time again, making the summer gatherings feel like family, rather than just another event to attend. The impartation of tangible, authentic love bears fruit that lasts beyond the yearly conferences, and spreads to communities at home and beyond.

We live in a day and time when people are said to be lovers of self and money, and where more time is spent surfing social media and connecting remotely than face to face. So much calls our attention away from God. At the same time, there is much online to feed our souls. At any time, and almost from anywhere, we can tune into Spirit-filled teachings and amazing worship. We can watch videos of healings, and log onto sites to receive prophetic words. There is an ample feast of this for English speakers, and it would be easy to be satisfied with our own custom made agenda of preferred spiritual food, all with an online community of people who agree with our designer faith. There is great opportunity there. But there is also great danger.

It is too easy to surf from site to site, online church to online church, video to video, and never become deeply rooted. A plethora of options abound, but they are accompanied by a growing loneliness and desperation for belonging. Statistics tell us that depression is increasing in the West. What is needed today is the reality of belonging that comes in a community committed to love, in the power of the Holy Spirit.

The fruit of the Spirit, especially love, is not something that can be picked up through online teachings, or even conferences, and be expected to last. The Spirit's fruit comes through a deeper process that requires time and investment. You cannot bear the fruit of the Spirit unless you are filled with the Spirit and connected to the body of Christ.

Many are still confused about, or unsure of, the Holy Spirit. The HSRM Conference provides clear, deep teachings on the Holy Spirit, the indwelling of the Spirit, and the gifts of the Spirit. Every year people receive greater insight, revelation, and confidence in what it means to be filled with the Spirit. In that process people are shown how to be rooted in love, and to pursue the things of the Spirit which will nurture their spiritual roots. These roots, when established in love, allow believers to mature and bear fruit. As Ephesians 3:17b-19 reads,

I pray that you,
being rooted and established in love,
may have power,
together with all the saints,
to grasp
how wide
and long
and high
and deep
is the love of Christ,
and to know this love that surpasses knowledge
—that you may be filled
to the measure of all the fullness of God.

Teaching people to be rooted and established in love provides a firm foundation for the full expression of God's love. Practically, this happens through teaching, modeling ways to spend personal time with God, and the reading of the Word of God. The filling of the Holy Spirit is not just something that takes place at a conference, but is a daily experience. Without this daily filling, the fruit does not mature and last.

Without being rooted and established in love, not only "are we nothing" (I Corinthians 13), but our good deeds, and our practicing of gifts, can be misdirected, misused, and even abusive. People with good intentions can do harm when they lack the foundation of love.

Another necessary teaching for equipping people in producing the fruit of love is a focus on disciplines, and the importance of allowing God to prune us. It is easy to just want the "feel good" part of the Holy Spirit's presence. But without the discipline of pruning, we become unruly vines spreading where we are not meant to go, and our fruit becomes bitter and distasteful to others. We must teach people to take time to allow the Holy Spirit to convict of sin, so we can confess, repent, and allow God to cut away things that hinder the expression of love. I see this happening in mentoring, praying, and conversing at HSRM conferences. This desire and commitment to see people mature and bear fruit is itself an authentic expression of love.

The core distinctive of love is demonstrated generously at HSRM conferences. The authenticity of this love is most evident when it lasts beyond the conference time and becomes a lifestyle. One summer after conference, my family and I stopped for a few days in Monroe, Michigan. After church at Redeemer Fellowship, a large group of us went to lunch at a local restaurant where our son was employed. One of the HSRM Conference speakers had challenged us to love tangibly, sharing how he tips people generously. When it came time to pay the lunch bill, two of our party gave a very generous tip to the waitress. She burst into tears when she saw it, because that was exactly what she needed that day. It covered her immediate need, and gave her a clear demonstration of God's love for her.

Love is not just a teaching or a good story at a conference. Our lunch group did not walk away impressed with the lavish tips. The love of God is not just a good feeling. It is a verb. A doing. Love is a lifestyle. To truly love is to live every day in response to God's love for us. The filling of the Holy Spirit equips and empowers us to live this way, and bear much fruit.

HSRM is built on a foundation of authentic love. But it is not taken for granted. The leaders and many wonderful speakers have exhorted us to love well. They have modeled love through impartation, so that the gifts would not stay with the receiver but be passed on to others. This kind of teaching and training has enriched the core family of HSRM to grow in love and in practice.

Young people especially are looking for authentic love. They are not interested in formal religious activity, and quickly become bored by spiritual spas. Once they leave a conference, or even church, and go back to their daily challenges, they need to be equipped to allow God to work through them in love.

As Hebrews 10:24 says, *"Let us consider how we may spur one another on toward love and good deeds."* This equipping comes through teaching, training, and impartation, which is then followed by opportunities for practice. The practice of love in action fans the flame, building confidence so that it will continue to make an impact once the conference is over.

I witnessed love in action at the conference in 2018. The youth and young adults went out of their way to go into the town of Green Lake, Wisconsin, to seek out people and bless them in love. They came back excited with testimonies of how God worked through them. The whole HSRM family rejoiced with them, and all were encouraged to continue this demonstration of love in our own communities.

Equipping the family of God to make time in our busy lives to share the love with our neighbors is essential if we want our spiritual gifts to grow and mature in love. Mark 12:33 instructs us,

And there is something more important to God
than all the sacrifices and burnt offerings:
it's the commandment to constantly love God
with every passion of your heart,
with your every thought,
and with all your strength
— and to love your neighbor
in the same way as you love yourself.
(The Passion Translation)

Love is a core distinctive of HSRM. I have seen and experienced it tangibly, year after year. The family of HSRM follows the new command of Jesus well: *Love one another. As I have loved you, so you must love one another.* (John 13:34, NIV)

Such love is contagious. The attractiveness of a Spirit-filled movement like HSRM is not the speakers, gifts, signs, and wonders. It is the authentic love of God, demonstrated through a humble people of God, who have formed a family. This family generously adopts others, as all are welcome. This family is built on a foundation of love. From there this love multiplies to reach our neighbors at the conference, and overflows to our homes, neighbors, communities, cities, and across the world.

After my first HSRM Conference in 2008, the funding came through as committed. NightLight was able to purchase a building in a red-light area of Bangkok. The vision for this building was an outreach center to reach a dark and broken neighborhood with the love of God.

Two groups from HSRM came to Thailand to do some work on the building. One night, Pastor John Piippo and Jon Standifer sat on boxes in the gutted ground floor of the building, in the heart of the red light area, and played their guitars for the Lord. A man came to the door and asked if he could come in with his beer to listen. We welcomed him, he lingered for some time. Pastor John began to speak with him, and before long the man was crying and receiving prayer. As he left, he turned to us and said, "Thank you for letting me bring my beer into church."

The vision of using this building to impact a dark neighborhood with love was already coming true through this team from HSRM! The love which is core to HSRM had made its way across the world to Bangkok. This divine love is an active response to the love we have experienced from God through the Holy Spirit's filling. For the fruit of the Spirit is Love!

2

PASSION FOR GOD
ED OWENS

Perhaps you have experienced the ups and downs of the Christian life. At times you are filled with vitality and enthusiasm for God. You are focused on loving God and loving others, to the glory of God. But then come some down times. You are drained of energy, low on desire for things of the Spirit. You operate more out of "ought" than passion for the things of God. I have been in both places.

The Holy Spirit Renewal Conference has played a significant role in my spiritual cycle —the up cycle! I recall one year when I attended the conference. I arrived with hopes of refreshing. The extended times of worship helped me focus on God. I began to weep as I experienced the real presence of God. I was being renewed!

One morning, early in the week, the speaker, Randy Clark, took time to pray blessing and impartation over individuals in the auditorium. Randy worked his way down the lines of people who came to the front, laying hands on each person. Trailing him were two HSRM leaders. They, too, were praying over individuals. People were being dramatically touched by the presence of the Spirit.

I am not a person given to emotional expression, but something was happening that evening at the conference. When one of the HSRM leaders laid hands on my forehead, God visited me in a unique and powerful way. I experienced God's power, physically and emotionally. This was unlike anything I had previously encountered. It was so intense that I began to wonder if I could survive God's holy presence. I did! I felt tremendously renewed, ready again for ministry.

Though this spiritual cycle of ups and downs seems normal and to be expected, I don't think we should settle for it. A cyclical gaining and losing passion for God is not what God desires.

In our common human lives a loss of focus and passion happens. For example, in the spring of 2018 we Detroit Tigers fans began the season with renewed hope and great expectation. This would be the year we win the World Series! But slowly, over the season, injuries mounted, players were traded away, and more games were lost than won. Even die-hard enthusiasts found their hopes dashed. I hate to be a fair-weather fan, but even I lost interest in watching Tiger baseball! That can be expected and accepted when it comes to sports. But should it be normal for the Christian life? Should we tolerate a cyclical passion for Almighty God that rises and diminishes? I think not.

In Romans 12:1 Paul describes the Christian life using temple terminology. Every Jew would have been familiar with the sacrificial system in the Jerusalem temple. In their minds they could picture animals being hoisted onto the altar for sacrifice to God, as acts of worship, and for cleansing of their sin. In that context Paul describes the Christian life. "I appeal to you therefore, brothers, by the mercies of God, to present your bodies as a living sacrifice, holy and acceptable to God, which is your spiritual worship." (ESV)

I remember my beginning as a follower of Jesus. I was excited! Life was now in color. I was going to live all-out for Jesus. My entire self was on the altar. I wanted to do great things in the service of my King. Do you remember your original passion for God?

But then the doldrums arrived, interrupting my spiritual fervency. Is this what God desired for me, as one of his children? Does this bring glory to God?

I believe God has a different intention for his children. God wants us to live with consistent passion for him. I have seen this reality lived by leaders of HSRM, even though most others I know seem dominated by the ebb and flow of renewal. This is the heartbeat of the mission of HSRM. Our greatest desire is to see people, and churches, live with passion for God through the power and presence of the Holy Spirit. Is this possible?

"BOIL IN THE SPIRIT!"

To answer that question let's explore Romans 12:11. The English Standard Version translates this as: "Do not be slothful in zeal, be fervent in spirit, serve the Lord." If you study the original Greek language you discover that this verse commands two things. First, we are told not to be lazy as believers called to serve Jesus. Secondly, we are, literally, to "boil" in spirit or in the Spirit.

Let's look at this command *to boil*. This can either refer to our human spirit, or to our life in the Holy Spirit. Either way, we are commanded to boil. What in the world does God mean by that word?

Here's what it doesn't mean. Boiling in the Spirit does *not* mean we are to maintain a constant emotional high. While emotions are not to be despised, they are not the measure of discipleship. If they were, then emotionally expressive types would make better disciples, and emotionally unexpressive personalities would make lousy disciples. Emotions come and go as we respond to stimuli from our environment. Emotions are hard to maintain. Strong emotions can deplete our energy quickly.

"Boiling in the Spirit" involves more than just our emotions. This is about passion for God. Webster's Dictionary has several definitions for the word 'passion.' One is: "Object of desire or deep interest." So, while passion may include emotion, it suggests priority and focus. Jesus tells us to "seek *first* the kingdom." (Matthew 6:33) This indicates that the kingdom, the rule and reign of Jesus, is our first priority. We must focus on his ways and his will. So, keep doing this. Boil in the Spirit!

This is neither easy nor automatic. The early church needed the command of Romans 12:11 as much as we do today. This is evident in the seven letters in Revelation to the churches of Asia (modern day Turkey). For example, the church of Ephesus had several positive attributes. They were zealous for correct doctrine. They did not tolerate theological laziness or heretical teachers. They were an active church, known for many loving, good works. But one thing was missing. It was so serious that Jesus threatened to take away their lamp stand if they did not repent. What was it that they had lost? They had abandoned their first love (Revelation 2:4). This was about their passion for their Lord. Doing church and ministry had replaced their devotion for Jesus. Their passion, their focus, needed reigniting. They needed to "boil in the Spirit" again.

The church of Laodicea was in a wealthy city. The town had financed an aqueduct that extended a considerable distance to some hot springs. The hot mineral springs were considered healthy for bathing. So, the enterprising folks of Laodicea set out to import hot water to their fair city. Imagine the chagrin of the city engineers when the hot spring water arrived in Laodicea the first time, only to discover that it had cooled to lukewarmness. Cold water and hot water were desired in their culture, but not lukewarm. This undesirable liquid served as an analogy for the failing of that church to heed the command of scripture to "boil in the Spirit." (Revelation 3:15-16)

As I have had the privilege of traveling to various churches as part of my work, I have discovered good people. They are committed to their community, and their church. Though many of these churches are in decline, they are invested in the survival of their congregation. But what I have often not witnessed are people who "boil in the Spirit" when it comes to their worship or conversation about the Lord.

Here is why this is important to me. This summer I took a bike trip across the Upper Peninsula of Michigan. We started in the tip of the Keweenaw Peninsula, where it juts into Lake Superior. For six days we rode our bicycles over the hills until we reached Paradise, Michigan. I had great fellowship with five other men. But as the week was ending I began to look forward to returning home to my wife, Sherry. I began to think about what kind of reception I would receive when I returned home. I am not expecting Sherry to worship me, but she loves me and usually drops whatever she is doing to greet me with hugs and kisses. But what if, when I returned home from a trip, her response was "Oh, you're here." And perhaps adding, "Would you take out the garbage?" A mutual, whole-hearted loving response feels better than what would seem like half-hearted indifference.

Imagine how it is with God if I half-heartedly worship him. Is God honored when I live distractedly, hardly reflecting on God's presence and activity in my life? Passion for God brings honor to him. He deserves and expects me to honor him by "boiling in the Spirit." Ho-hum to God just doesn't cut it.

This is supremely important because it concerns spreading God's kingdom. When Jesus departed this world to take his seat at the right hand of the Father, he commanded his disciples to go and make more disciples. But who would desire to join some kingdom populated with unpassionate people? Who will join our churches if we neglect obeying his commands to make disciples, and to boil in the Spirit?

I have several earthly things I am passionate about; bicycle touring is one of them. It has not been a burden to passionately talk to others about this. Because of my passionate attitude, I have had others join me on bicycle trips. By the same reasoning, others will be influenced when God's people honor him with their passion.

The command to "boil in the Spirit" is so important because it is just that—a command. This is not a heavenly suggestion. This is what we earthly creatures owe to our loving creator.

"DON'T BE LAZY!"

I recently retired. I determined I was going to work on increasing my health by regularly going to the gym. I figured that going every other day should improve my health, and perhaps lengthen the days of my life. The gym is only a couple blocks down the road from where we live. It is convenient, so going regularly should be no problem. That's the theory. But the reality looks like this. There is always something that comes up, some reason not to go today. But mostly my problem is laziness.

It is hard to keep boiling in the Spirit. Perhaps I am expecting God, or someone or something else, to take care of the problem for me. But, part of the problem is laziness. We are unwilling to expend serious work at keeping ourselves boiling in the Spirit.

A command implies responsibility. I have a part in tending the fires of the Spirit. I must get out of the recliner and exercise unto godliness. I have discovered that God doesn't give me commands that frustrate me because they could never be fulfilled.

To illustrate, imagine that I took my four-year-old grandson to the Breslin Center, home of the Michigan State University Spartans. It is half-time of the game. I have somehow convinced the authorities to allow my grandson to entertain the crowd during the intermission. I stand at center court, and yell with my most authoritative voice, "Caleb, dunk the basketball!" Caleb, however, is incapable of leaping over ten feet high to slam the ball through the nylon net. My command is therefore ridiculous, because there is no hope of compliance. Caleb could run to the basket and jump a tiny bit off the ground. If I were waiting at the hoop, I could scoop him up and lift him over my head so he could dunk the basketball. In that scenario I would have a big role in fulfilling the command, but still he can do his part.

In God's command to boil in the Spirit, I don't know how much depends on me, and how much is God's gracious work. But I do know I need to stop being lazy, and focus on staying passionate about loving, worshiping, and serving God.

HOW CAN I KEEP BOILING?

One of my favorite recreational activities is combining bicycle touring with camping. I have a couple bags (panniers) waiting in my closet to clip onto a rack on my bicycle, so I can take off at a moment's notice. In those packs I have a lightweight tent and sleeping bag. I also have a small stove, called a Pocket Rocket. I can screw the mini-stove into a small propane canister, and boil water in a small, lightweight pot. Soon my meal is boiling. That works fine for bike camping, but I doubt you want me to try and use that to get you boiling in the Spirit.

What can I do if I quit being lazy, and try to obey the command? Let me suggest a few practices which help me keep boiling. I am going to borrow heavily on some teaching that Dr. John Piippo has spoken about at the Holy Spirit Renewal Conference.

First, soaking in God's Word helps us stay passionate about God. There is an inverse relationship between a lack of Bible reading and meditation, and our spiritual condition. People who soak themselves in the Scripture with a humble, open heart, tend to grow and boil. People who neglect God's Word are less likely to be on fire for the Lord. I need to carve out time to daily read and listen to what God is saying to me. The Bible reveals to me the greatness of God and his gracious work of salvation. While I read, allowing God's truths to soak into my heart, the Spirit draws me into a deeper, more focused walk with him.

Secondly, we need to renew our communication with God. This deepens our intimacy with him. This unleashes "rivers of water" into our lives (Jesus identifies these waters as the Spirit in John 7:38,39) It is interesting that we often repeat the Lord's Prayer, but forget one of the most important petitions connected to it. We analyze the requests of Jesus's model, but forget that he gives a specific thing to request. If you read further in Luke 11 you discover an important petition.

> *"What father among you, if his son asks for a fish, will instead of a fish give him a serpent; or if he asks for an egg, will give him a scorpion? If you then, who are evil, know how to give good gifts to your children, how much more will the heavenly Father give the Holy Spirit to those who ask him!"* (Luke 11: 11-12, ESV)

We need more of the Holy Spirit! We need more of his power and presence in our lives. As God himself takes up intimate residency in us, we begin to heat up spiritually. We must consciously and consistently ask for the gift of the Holy Spirit. As he comes, he will impart spiritual fruit, gifts, empowerment for witnessing, boldness, desire for fellowship, a heart of worship, and much more. Keep praying! We need more of the Holy Spirit!

Finally, hanging around others who are boiling helps us to stay passionate toward the Lord. Some time ago I realized the value of surrounding myself with people who have a desire to grow and serve with passion. Three of us began to meet weekly, sharing from our journals what God is doing and saying as we meditate on scripture and pray. Then we pray specifically for each other. This provides accountability, and great encouragement. We sharpen one another in our pursuit of God. Conversely, if your church environment lacks passion for God, it can have a negative impact on you. This makes it important to find friends to journey with you in seeking to boil in the Spirit.

It is time to shed the characteristic of laziness. It is time to fulfill the command of Romans 12:11 to "boil in the Spirit."

Respond joyfully to Jesus's command.

Go and boil!

3

THE HOLY SPIRIT GETS US OUT OF THE BOAT
ROSS LLEWELLAN

And Peter answered him. "Lord, if it is you, command me to come to you on the water." He said, "Come." So Peter got out of the boat and walked on the water and came to Jesus; but when he saw the wind, he was afraid, and beginning to sink he cried out, "Lord, save me." Jesus immediately reached out his hand and caught him, saying to him, "O man of little faith, why did you doubt?" And when they got into the boat, the wind ceased. And those in the boat worshiped him, saying, "Truly you are the Son of God."
Matthew 14: 28-33

A couple of summers ago I floated the Bighorn River in Montana with some friends. The Bighorn River is one of the area's greatest blue ribbon trout fishing rivers. Our raft could hold three comfortably, and sat fairly high on the water.

We guided the raft over to shallow water to get out. I put one leg over the side. Simple enough. "This will be easy," I thought. I then realized the river bottom was further down than expected. I couldn't touch bottom! I quickly tried to swing my other leg over and out of the raft. This would enable me to hit the river feet-first in knee deep water.

But there was a problem. My other leg got caught in the raft. Now I had one leg out of the raft, and the other stuck inside. My weight had shifted, so I had most of my body out of the raft, with the other leg stuck inside. My posterior was almost touching the water. I didn't have the strength to pull myself back into the raft. Where was my gymnastic gift when I needed it? Probably, it ceased with the apostles!

If you can't picture this scene, that's okay. It wasn't a pretty picture. I was trying to be graceful, and just hang in there. I couldn't figure out if I should try to pull myself back into the raft or fall into the river. It was not a deep plunge, but I would have to get wet.

The day was hot. I chose the fall. And, yes, my friend and his son were scrambling, not to help, but for their cameras. I'm sure they couldn't wait to get this on Facebook!

I'm not good at getting out of boats and rafts. How about you? Are you good at getting out of your boat? If your boat is your comfort zone, how are you at getting out of that? If you are like me, probably not very good! We all have challenges of faith and risk. But God has a way of calling us to more, doesn't he?

There was a time in my life when I would have never gotten out of my comfortable boat and become associated with a ministry centered on being renewed and baptized in the Holy Spirit. But here I am. Jesus called me out of my comfort zone. And I have been involved in Holy Spirit Renewal Ministries for over twenty-five years.

During my college days, in the 1970s, I had a negative experience with "Charismatics." I wanted nothing to do with Charismatic/Pentecostal leanings. But God has a sense of humor. The first church I accepted in Oregon after seminary was, unknown to me, filled with wonderful people who either had, or desired, deeper experiences in the Holy Spirit.

I went on a retreat called the "Walk to Emmaus" in the late 1980s and experienced a profound encounter with Jesus healing me. The Walk to Emmaus is a three-day retreat where talks, small groups, meditations, healing services, and a variety of fellowship times are designed to allow a person to receive more of God's love. It was at a healing service that I went forward. I asked to be prayed over to remove fears from my life. I experienced an overwhelming sense of peace and freedom. I sensed that fears were taken from my life, and from that moment on, I wanted more of the Spirit's power and gifts to flow in my life. It was a work of God's grace to give me that desire. I believe Jesus called me out of my comfortable theological boat to greater understanding and appreciation of the power and gifts of the Holy Spirit.

I always believed that all the gifts of the Holy Spirit described in the pages of Scripture were valid. But I never personally sought for gifts like tongues, prophecies, or healing. That is, until I experienced that encounter with the Spirit on the Walk to Emmaus. Now I wanted all God had for me, and for the church!

I began to experience tongues, praying for other's healings, giving encouraging prophecies to people, as well as witnessing authentic demonstrations of the Spirit coming upon people. At the time I didn't plan to desire "more." It just happened! But Jesus knew what he was doing. He was calling me out of my boat.

Enter HSRM. As a committed American Baptist pastor, I attended many conferences and retreats, but knew nothing about this exciting ministry within our own denominational family. I called Dr. Gary Clark, who was chairperson of HSRM, because I wanted to know more about this organization that emphasized the power and freedom of the Holy Spirit. The rest is, as they say, history. Over twenty-five years ago we attended, for the first time, the HSRM Conference in Green Lake, Wisconsin. Now I am privileged to be part of the leadership team.

As I reflect on my years with HSRM, three themes stand out. First, I am grateful for the way God has led us to lead others. Second, I am thankful God calls us to experience more. And third, I am captured by what I call "prophetic steps."

GRATITUDE FOR LEADERS.

HSRM has been blessed with leaders who have been called to get out of their theological and spiritual boats. Hebrews 13:7 counsels us to "Remember your leaders, who spoke the word of God to you; consider the outcome of their way of life, and imitate their faith."

I am to honor and follow leadership examples that have gone before me. So, I express my indebtedness to the many Christlike leaders who desired more of the Holy Spirit. They responded to Jesus's call to get out of their comfortable boats, and experience and know the Spirit's presence and ministry more deeply.

The American Baptist Charismatic Fellowship, now called Holy Spirit Renewal Ministries, was founded in the mid-1970s. Many have referred to the late 1960s and the 1970s as the birth and growth of the Charismatic Movement. The Holy Spirit was poured out upon many people, in many denominations. HSRM is a product of that.

People were desiring gifts, expressions, and demonstrations of the Spirit. Many within our American Baptist churches responded to this outpouring. They wanted a conference to express their freedom in the Spirit that, often, their home churches neither welcomed, nor wanted. Out of this beginning, HSRM emerged.

To be part of something like this, in a historic denomination, was not easy in those days. Many of our leaders paid a price for getting out of the boat and testing these spiritual waters. Many suffered scorn and misunderstanding. I know of several who were dismissed from their churches because expressions of the Spirit were not allowed to happen.

But this was not all about suffering. They were witnessing new things God was doing. New churches were being born in many places. I myself have had the privilege of pastoring two churches that were birthed, and renewed, by leaders associated with HSRM.

Churches were growing and experiencing God's renewing Spirit. Lives were being transformed. There were supernatural healings, gifts of the Spirit, and, above all, many were brought into the Kingdom. I stand on their shoulders! They were risk-takers who followed Jesus, desiring outpourings of the Spirit upon their lives.

Someone has said that structure does not bring life, but where there is life, build structure. Out of these many experiences of new life, our visionary forbearers saw the need to organize HSRM. They had faith to build structure that would steward the outpouring of the Spirit. They began developing leaders to handle this growing movement. They desired to make a difference, both in our denomination, and in the Body of Christ.

Those leaders didn't just gather to enjoy each other's company at Green Lake each summer. They were responding to God's call to further something he was doing, now, and for future generations. They didn't always know what God had in mind for this burgeoning ministry. But they got out of their boats, committing themselves to more!

Perhaps we think creating a structure is not a big deal. Some believe organization will quench the Spirit. However, I look at this as a huge "get out of the boat" step. Leadership structures were put in place that would ensure this ministry would last through the years.

I've seen several movements of God's people eventually lose focus and energy and die out. I've seen churches close their doors. I don't know all the "whys" of ministries that once looked promising but lost focus and purpose. I praise God that HSRM leaders, from the beginning, had vision, sought the Holy Spirit's direction, *and* were led to provide a life-giving ministry that would last beyond them!

Many sacrificed time, money, and ministry skills as God was blessing this new movement. They were willing to bless HSRM with all God had given them. I appreciate that! HSRM has been able to offer resources and help for pastors and churches desiring renewal, as well as be a beacon of hope to our American Baptist denomination.

Most of HSRM's leadership has emerged from the American Baptist family. These are leaders who desired, for American Baptists, the restoration of the Holy Spirit's power, gifts, and times of refreshing. And, along the way, God has widened the scope of HSRM to include many flavors of folks seeking renewal in the Spirit. Many Spirit-seekers from different backgrounds have joined us.

When I began to hunger for more of the Spirit in my life I was surprised to find that American Baptists had an organization committed to the power of the Holy Spirit in a believer's life. Though HSRM had already existed for years, I discovered it in the late 1980s. When that happened, I felt like I had discovered gold!

HSRM is a gold mine, a unique deposit of God's presence with us, as we come together at Green Lake. I am richer in Christ for being part of this. I remain grateful for those who got out of their boats, believing they were called to more. I honor them, giving thanks to the One from whom every good and perfect gift flows.

CALLED TO MORE

In Matthew 14 we see the disciples on the lake, in their boat. Jesus comes to them, walking on the water. Peter says to Jesus, "Lord, if that's you, tell me to come to you on the water." Jesus says, "Come," thus confirming Peter's desire. What were you thinking, Jesus, inviting Peter out on the water?

I have always wondered why Peter asked to get out of the boat. Was it his impulsiveness? Was he trying to prove his "faith" to others? Was he prompted by the Holy Spirit to experience more in his walk with Jesus? I believe the latter more aptly describes his motive.

I suppose there are those who think Jesus was setting Peter up for a fall. Perhaps Jesus invited Peter on the water, knowing he would sink, and then save him to teach him a lesson. I don't see Jesus doing this. Rather, the lesson Jesus taught Peter was, "In my power and strength, water-walking can happen."

Peter *did* walk on the water and come to Jesus! Why this event? I believe Jesus was inviting Peter to "more." This was an offer to experience…
…more of the miraculous,
…more of Jesus' peace in that morning storm,
…more adventure in his walk!

Getting out of the boat had further implications for Peter. The experience on the Sea of Galilee that morning was a training session for future ministry opportunities. It would prepare him for times when he would be led by the Spirit to get out of the boat to preach on the day of Pentecost (Acts 2). Later on, Peter sensed God's call through the vision of the unclean animals and got out of his Jewish comfort zone to bring the gospel to the Gentiles (Acts 10). Those two experiences were truly "getting out of the boat" moments!

What could that mean for me? For you? I have found that Jesus is always calling me to more growth in him, and to further experience the presence and power of the Holy Spirit in and through me. Do any of us think we have come to a place where we fully know and have experienced it all? I hardly think so.

Paul put it this way: "Not that I have already obtained this or am already perfect; but I press on to make it my own, because Christ Jesus has made me his own" (Philippians 3:12, ESV). Even the apostle Paul knew there was "more" for him in his journey with Christ. So, I am open to his invitation to come out on the water and go places I have never been before.

HSRM has been a place where I have been called to "more." Surely, I feel called to more every day as I encounter challenges that stretch me beyond my comfort zone. Being involved as a leader on our HSRM team has provided opportunities to get out of my comfort zone.

I have discovered new leadership roles that have called me to more teaching, prayer, and training others. When I accepted a call to be on the HSRM leadership team, I gladly said "Yes," not fully realizing all that God was calling me to.

Through the years I have experienced being renewed in greater joy. I have gained more than I ever thought possible. Each time this involved the call of Jesus to get out of my boat, accompanied by a desire to do so. For example, this happened one night at our conference. This might seem trivial to you, but it was a significant step for me.

In our conference sessions HSRM has a way of transitioning from our guest speaker to eliciting response from the people gathered there. This allows the listening community to be a discerning community, as together we share our sense of what the Spirit is saying and doing. Dr. Clay Ford, one of our executive committee leaders, often handles those transitions. Clay has a unique gift of doing this seamlessly.

One night, as our speaker was presenting, Clay came to me. He said he wasn't feeling well. "Would you," he asked, "facilitate the transition tonight?"

I remember not being thrilled with this speaker. I'm sure the speaker was saying some inspiring things, but I was not into it. Maybe I had a bad golf game that afternoon and was still stuck on the course!

I prayed for Clay's healing, hoping that would take care of his question. I didn't want to be the transition person. To my disappointment Clay was not healed instantaneously. So I said, "I'll do it." I didn't want to look like a wimpy leader. But truthfully, I didn't know what to do!

I prayed silently. God didn't download some unique "word" to me of how we should respond as a conference to what the speaker was doing. For some reason, after the message, having an altar call for healing prayer just didn't seem the right thing to do. As I walked up to get the microphone, I felt weird. I am no stranger to speaking in front of crowds, but this time felt different. It felt like, you guessed it, getting out of the boat.

In retrospect I see the Lord, and Clay, setting me up for this one. "Okay, Jesus, if you are asking me to do this, what am I to do? How should I lead this brief time of transition and response?" I was being called to more of what the Spirit wanted to do at that moment!

Since the speaker's message was more introspective in nature, I led in a time of quiet meditation and confession of sin. The atmosphere became still and quiet. People were dealing with stuff that needed to be addressed with God.

Why am I writing about this story? Here's why. It's in times when I am asked to do something that doesn't fit my style, and what I am accustomed to doing, that I may be called to "more." Have you ever prayed for a person in public and you're not the public, prayin' type? What about witnessing to a friend about the love of Christ, and you can barely get the words out of your mouth? What if someone asks you to lead a ministry you have very little desire or skill for? It's in those times that we should wonder if this is the Lord, calling us to water-walk. Such times require more dependence on him, rather than on our own abilities and experience. I expect that God will continue to call me to more. As this happens, I will again be getting out of my boat.

PROPHETIC STEPS

When Peter stepped out of the boat, at the call of Jesus, he took a prophetic step. The entire experience that morning on the Sea of Galilee was an experiment for Peter's future. Peter only saw the present: risking to get out of the boat, the success of walking on water, the immersion (yes, Peter was a Baptist), and Jesus' faithfulness at that moment. What Peter didn't realize at the time was what Jesus knew about his future.

Getting out of the boat that morning was a prophetic step that Peter would relive, many times in the days ahead, only on dry land. He would eventually be called out of his familiar life on the Day of Pentecost to preach to thousands. He wasn't counting on getting out of the boat do that. (Acts 2:14-36)

Once, on his way to the Temple, Peter saw a lame man. He didn't expect to say anything. But again, prompted by the Holy Spirit, he stepped out and said to the man: "Silver or gold I do not have, but what I do have I give you. In the name of Jesus Christ of Nazareth, walk." (Acts 3:6)

When Peter was commanded by Jewish authorities to stay in his comfort zone and stop preaching in the name of Jesus, he refused and, filled with the Holy Spirit, boldly proclaimed: "Which is right in God's eyes: to listen to you, or to him? You be the judges! As for us, we cannot help speaking about what we have seen and heard." (Acts 4: 19-20)

Peter would be called out of yet another comfort zone----his Jewish tradition. This happened as he went to a roof top to pray. Suddenly, God gave him a vision of unclean animals, with an invitation to share Jesus and the gospel with non-Jews. So, Peter walked on the water to befriend Gentiles, realizing they also were worthy of the Gospel. (Acts 10)

Are you getting the picture? The event on the Sea of Galilee was not just an isolated, once-in-a-lifetime experience. Peter was being prepared for a lifestyle of boat-leaving and water-walking.

I have found that, in following Jesus, one simple, risky step today often prepares me for bigger steps tomorrow. We all started with a first step as we stepped out of the boat. I had no idea where this would take me, or how God would use this to lead to more impactful victories or ministries. Like the early leaders of HSRM experienced, these steps were prophetic.

I see this happening all the time, even when I don't recognize it. I had to respond to the call to preach and teach, which at first was risky both for me and the church. Many of my brothers and sisters had to take a first step and pray for the sick. It seemed different, but now praying for others has become a lifestyle. If you are a vocalist or musician, it had to start somewhere. It was a step of faith, and you were nervous. Yet, you responded to the voice of Jesus. God used a continual "getting out of your boat" to train you for a greater ministry.

What is your comfort zone now? Maybe, just maybe, God is calling you into his kingdom zone to prepare you for greater, wider, more impactful ministries? Today's "out of my comfort zone" prepares me for tomorrow's victory.

Permit me to share one more story that always inspires me. A man invited his friend to come to the desert in Southern California. This man shared his vision with his friend. He saw a theme park "out in the sand." He saw hotels and restaurants. He saw a place where families would come to enjoy vacations. He was willing to risk. He asked his friend to invest his money with him. His friend refused. By now you've gathered that this man was none other than Walt Disney. And his friend? A man by the name of Art Linkletter. (Linkletter was a well-known radio and television personality in the 1940s and 50s. Linkletter later wrote of his regret at not investing in Disney's vision.)

I'm grateful that those early leaders of HSRM saw more than just a passing spiritual fad, or another summer vacation. They risked getting out of their boats, trusting Jesus to sustain them on the water.

Do you see your first steps today as prophetic? If not, be encouraged. What God is calling you to today is significant. I believe those steps are prophetic, and that God will use them to train you for greater ministry, as he did for Peter.

Jesus calls us out of our comfort zones for a greater journey, which blesses him, and will bless others. Be faithful to hear his voice. Will you get out of your boat?

4

THE HOLY SPIRIT AND HEALING
TERI NYBERG

Every year, for the past twenty-five years, I have made an eight-hour journey to one of my favorite places on earth, Green Lake Conference Center in Green Lake, Wisconsin. I travel to attend and experience the week-long Holy Spirit Renewal Ministries Conference. This yearly conference takes place around the last week of June.

Arriving at the conference center, we pull up to a tall brick gate on Highway 23. This opens into a beautiful green area with a golf course on both sides. A couple of old, distinguished looking houses appear, and I feel a peace coming over me. It's all so familiar.

We travel down a paved, winding path. Taking turns with the cars coming towards us, we cross a quaint, one-car bridge. Moving on, we drive through a wooded area. The trees are tall and thick. They arch over, touching trees on both sides of the road, forming a "tree tunnel." We often see deer in this area. They are beautiful and graceful, adding to the experience.

As we emerge from the wooded covering, there it is: the Conference Center. I see boats, bikes, paddle boats, pontoons, and a beach for swimming. Ahead on the left is Pillsbury Hall, a large meeting room on the shores of the lake. It is here that I have heard so many wonderful, well-known speakers, and learned so much about the Holy Spirit and the gifts of the Spirit.

To the right is Kraft Hall, where we register, eat, and fellowship around the dinner table. Next door and down the road are sleeping accommodations - cabins, houses, and motel rooms. It is all familiar and exciting. I get this sense every year. It's like coming home again!

I feel the same every time I come to Green Lake. Here, at this conference, I have watched God move in miraculous ways, big and small, and always amazing. I believe I see God's Spirit in action because of my high expectations and anticipation. I guess you would call that faith. I have faith that God is going to touch people's lives. And he does!

I have this sense of "home" because of the people I am going to be with. I have reunited with the same group of people, for one glorious week in the summer, year after year. Actually, they are more than just a group of people, and more than friends. You will hear this phrase more than once in this book: "They are family."

This spiritual family is united by the Holy Spirit that dwells within us. When we come together for this wonderful week, it is not a conference *about the Holy Spirit*. Rather, the entire week is an *encounter with the Holy Spirit*. It is a moment in time to reset, get back on track, and experience continuing relationship with the Holy Spirit. One thing I have learned at this conference is this: the encounter with God's Spirit does not have to end!

Some years I have arrived empty and needing to be filled, only to be met by those who will pray for me and encourage me. There are several peaceful and quiet places where I can get alone with God, read my Bible, and just listen for his voice. Other years I arrive full of faith, ready to share, pray, and impart to others who need a fresh touch from God. The wonderful thing about our relationship with God is that he meets us where we are, and that there is always more to learn and receive.

My love for this conference began twenty-five years ago. I was attending First Baptist Church in Sioux Falls, South Dakota. This fellowship was a warm, Bible-believing church, with a rich history of community involvement, mission giving, and powerful prayer groups. It was traditional and non-demonstrative in its style of worship. The congregants loved God, and one another. The worship consisted of beautiful hymns, accompanied by our amazing pipe organ.

One Sunday morning one of our leaders, Susan, asked if I would be interested in going to a conference with her. I agreed, and we bravely decided to attend the Holy Spirit Renewal Conference. While I was familiar with Charismatic churches, and the wonderful expressions of Spirit-filled worship, I wondered what a "Baptist Holy Spirit Conference" would look like.

I discovered that it was similar to other charismatic worship events. For me, it felt like a breath of fresh air, or should I say, fresh wind. There were people dancing, singing, clapping, and raising their hands to the worship songs. This was worship music that elicited expression, demanding a response. Joy and love emanated from the people. I knew these people loved my Jesus.

Susan and I took it all in, soaking up the entire experience. We sang loud! We clapped and raised our hands! We said "Amen" and "Hallelujah!" I remember thinking, "This is what heaven will be like when we are worshiping around the throne of God."

Since that time, over one hundred people from Sioux Falls have joined our group on a yearly trip to Green Lake. We have witnessed many miracles. Some years we have had only six with us, and other years we have had as many as thirty-five. We trust that whoever God wants to be there will be the ones to join us.

The most significant experience we had at that first conference was an encounter with the God who heals. Susan had been having problems with a lump on her throat. This was concerning to her, because a few years earlier she had thyroid surgery, and had a lump removed from her throat. She couldn't help wondering if it had returned.

One of the conference speakers was Mike Evans. He was a prayer minister, and trained people at the conference to pray healing prayers for others. One evening, at the end of the service, Mike had youth come forward to be the prayer ministry teams. Susan got brave and went forward. She was in the group where Mike and four teenaged boys were praying. I was visiting with someone, when I heard my friend shouting, "It's gone, it's gone!" I looked up to see Susan, full of joy, holding her neck. I saw four young men staring at her, with their mouths hanging open! I talked to one of the boys afterwards, and he said, "The lump just went in and was gone." They were as surprised as Susan was at this miracle that God performed right before their eyes.

I think this was as much to build the faith of these four young prayer ministers as it was to bless and heal Susan. Since that time, I have seen God move in many ways and in many lives, but I will never forget that special moment when God met Susan!

On the last day of that first conference we were at an outdoor service. The main leaders of HSRM, Gary Clark and Joe Atkinson, said they had a prophetic word for Susan and First Baptist Church of Sioux Falls. I remember this like it was yesterday! They invited her to come forward and prayed for the Holy Spirit to begin moving in our home church. The word they had was, "Do not get ahead of the Spirit, but do not lag behind the Spirit either. Walk so close to the Holy Spirit that you are in step with him, and next to what he is doing." We have referred to that word often over the years.

The second year we had another experience of healing. This time it was for Susan's daughter, Charity. She was suffering with a chronic physical illness, and agreed to join us for one day at the conference. Charity was in her early twenties, beautiful, thin, and frail. It was a battle for her to travel to Green Lake from St. Paul. In addition to fatigue, she experienced car problems on her way.

Charity arrived late in the evening, with plans to leave the next afternoon. We had great faith in what God was going to do for her in this short time. All day long Susan and I kept urging her to go forward for prayer at the end of the services. She kept saying that she did not feel she was supposed to do this. Susan and I were fervently praying that she would, but she never did.

We felt discouraged that Charity did not respond the way we thought she should. We would have a final lunch together, and then she would head home, not healed. She would be leaving no better off than when she came. But God had a plan.

The keynote speaker that year was Dean Sherman, from Youth With a Mission. He believed in the gifts of the Spirit, especially healing. Dean walked into the cafeteria where we were having that final lunch. He stood by the door for a few minutes, looking around. Then he came over and asked if he could sit with us, next to Charity.

We got to visiting, and Charity's story about her illness and struggles came out. We asked Dean if he would pray for her. He said he would love to. Dean got up and stood behind her. Putting his hands on her shoulders, he prayed a powerful prayer of healing, right there in the cafeteria. Susan and I still think the room shook a little bit!

When he finished praying, Charity had a glow on her face. Dean shared that when he came into the cafeteria he asked God where to sit. He felt the Holy Spirit was guiding him to sit at our table.

God had seen Charity and her illness, and sent the "main speaker" to sit with her. That spoke volumes to her!

Dean asked if he could have a picture of Charity. Susan, being the good mom that she is, had one and gave it to him. Dean told Charity that he would continue to pray for her every day. Experiences like these left no doubt in our minds that we would be returning often to Green Lake.

A year later we were back. Dean Sherman was back as well, as one of the speakers. We were delighted because he held a special place in our heart from the previous year.

After one of his talks Susan went to Dean and asked if he remembered her. He opened his Bible, took out Charity's picture, and said, "You're the mother of the girl I have been praying for every day for the last year." What a holy moment that was for us!

It has been a process, but Charity is now completely healed, happy, and married with two beautiful children. She is a powerful intercessor for her church, and for the city of Los Angeles. We believe it started the day God saw her need and sent Dean to pray for her.

After those first years we decided we needed this life and power in our church. We invited Mike Evans and his wife, Jane, to speak at a weekend renewal and healing conference at First Baptist in Sioux Falls. We were not sure who would attend, but we went for it!

A medium-sized crowd showed up. This was enough to get us up and going. Mike was wonderful at teaching different styles of prayer, encouraging us all to "do the things that Jesus did." We already had a couple of long-time prayer groups and a Wednesday night intercessory prayer group. God spoke through Mike, lighting a fire in us. We were to have a regular "healing service" and make ourselves available after Sunday services for anyone needing or wanting prayer.

Some of the basics Mike taught were things such as: pray with our eyes open so we can observe if the Spirit is touching the ones we were praying for; have Kleenex ready if tears come; and bring some mints for our breath. In addition to tears, we were to look for flickering eyelids, or an affirming nod.

Mike told us to ask the Holy Spirit how we should pray for a person, and then wait, and listen.

In addition to those basic nuts-and-bolts kind of things Mike gave us scriptural references as to why we have the right and authority to pray for healing. He demonstrated how to pray for healing, gave us a model, and encouraged us to be open to move with how the Spirit is leading. I remember him saying, "Listen to God with your spiritual ears while listening with your physical ears to what the person you are praying for is saying. Hear the need that is behind the prayer request." These instructions have been helpful over the years.

At the end of the weekend Mike asked if anyone would like to make a commitment to be a prayer minister. Around thirty people responded! It was a precious time. We sensed the tangible presence of the Holy Spirit as Mike and Jane went to each person individually, anointed us with oil, laid hands on us, and prayed over us.

Among those who went forward for prayer was my dearest friend, Gloria. I need to add that, since that time with Mike and Jane Evans, Gloria has not missed a single Holy Spirit Renewal Conference. She and I have gone every year for twenty-three years. And, at the young age of eighty-eight, she has driven every year!

Gloria enjoys the music, wonderful speakers, instructional workshops, and the fellowship. But the most precious aspect of the Green Lake Conference is seeing the Holy Spirit move and heal those in need.

This conference has always offered excellent teaching on healing the sick. The amazing thing is that God uses us! Over the years we have been privileged to be on the prayer teams after the evening service, putting into practice what we have learned. We have seen many healings - physical, emotional, and spiritual.

Reflecting on these experiences has convinced me that a core distinctive of HSRM is *healing prayer.* God's Word talks about Jesus doing this. We read, in Luke chapters ten and eleven, that Jesus gave his disciples a mandate to heal the sick. Ultimately, all followers of Jesus have the power, authority, and instruction to heal the sick in his name.

We have many biblical examples of this. All four Gospels record eyewitness accounts of *Jesus healing the sick.* For example,

- "Great crowds came to him, bringing the lame, the blind, the crippled, the mute and many others, and laid them at his feet; and he healed them." (Matthew 15:30)

- "They ran throughout that whole region and carried the sick on mats to wherever they heard he was. And wherever he went—into villages, towns or countryside—they placed the sick in the marketplaces. They begged him to let them touch even the edge of his cloak, and all who touched it were healed." (Mark 6:55-56)

- "On a Sabbath Jesus was teaching in one of the synagogues, and a woman was there who had been crippled by a spirit for eighteen years. She was bent over and could not straighten up at all. When Jesus saw her, he called her forward and said to her, "Woman, you are set free from your infirmity." Then he put his hands on her, and immediately she straightened up and praised God." (Luke 13:10-13)

- "[The blind man] replied, "The man they call Jesus made some mud and put it on my eyes. He told me to go to Siloam and wash. So I went and washed, and then I could see." (John 9:11)

In the gospels we read that Jesus gave the disciples *authority to heal the sick.*

- "Jesus called his twelve disciples to him and gave them authority to drive out impure spirits and to heal every disease and sickness." (Matthew 10:1)

- Jesus gave them instructions, "Heal the sick, raise the dead, cleanse those who have leprosy,[a] drive out demons. Freely you have received; freely give." (Matthew 10:8)

- "Calling the Twelve to him, he began to send them out two by two and gave them authority over impure spirits... They went out and preached that people should repent. They drove out many demons and anointed many sick people with oil and healed them." (Mark 6:7, 12-13)

- "When Jesus had called the Twelve together, he gave them power and authority to drive out all demons and to cure diseases." (Luke 9:1)

Finally, we see that *all* believers have authority, in Jesus' name, through the power of the Holy Spirit, to heal the sick.

- "Therefore go and make disciples of all nations, baptizing them in the name of the Father and of the Son and of the Holy Spirit, and teaching them to obey everything I have commanded you. And surely I am with you always, to the very end of the age." (Matthew 28:19-20)

- "Now Stephen, a man full of God's grace and power, performed great wonders and signs among the people." (Acts 6:8)

- "His father was sick in bed, suffering from fever and dysentery. Paul went in to see him and, after prayer, placed his hands on him and healed him." (Acts 28:8)

- "Is anyone among you sick? Let them call the elders of the church to pray over them and anoint them with oil in the name of the Lord. [15] And the prayer offered in faith will make the sick person well; the Lord will raise them up. If they have sinned, they will be forgiven." (James 5:14-15)

- "When the crowds heard Philip and saw the signs he performed, they all paid close attention to what he said. For with shrieks, impure spirits came out of many, and many who were paralyzed or lame were healed." (Acts 8:6-7)

After the Healing Conference at our church with Mike and Jane Evans, we saw God open many doors leading to opportunities to pray for the sick. These included:

- Launching a monthly healing service.

- Stationed prayer ministers in the front of the sanctuary available to pray after each service.

- A prayer shawl ministry was started. (Acts 19:12 – "So that even handkerchiefs and aprons that had touched him were taken to the sick, and their illnesses were cured...") We took prayer shawls to the sick in homes and the hospital, and prayed over the people.

- Plus, there were numerous other opportunities to meet with people privately and pray.

First Baptist of Sioux Falls has always been a strong praying church. But, as we have come to see, God always has more for us. These privileged times of prayer for the sick were started because of the fire that was ignited in our hearts at that first Holy Spirit Conference.

Equipping and empowering people to pray for healing is something God wants to do in all churches. It just takes two willing people to begin praying for this. Talk to your pastors, share your vision with them, and then pray some more. Most pastors will welcome more prayer in their church. Once God opens a door, walk through it, and be willing to pray for those God brings to you. If you are available, and your pastor knows he can trust you, people will call on you for prayer. This has been my experience. Here is one more example.

Lois was an intelligent woman in her fifties. She ran her own accounting firm. One day at work she had a brain aneurysm. We were called to go to the hospital and pray for her. We secured a prayer shawl, and off we went.

We anointed her with oil, covered her with the shawl, and prayed for healing. Her situation was not looking good. We encouraged Lois to keep having people pray for her. We have discovered that sometimes God heals immediately, and other times he heals over a period of time. We visited Lois again, and prayed a few more times while she was in the hospital. As far as I could tell, she was not getting better.

One Sunday night, as we were having our monthly healing service in the chapel, wouldn't you know - Lois came walking in! She was going after her healing. She wanted prayer, and said she would be back every time we had a healing service. And eventually she was healed!

Lois was persistent. She kept filling us in on her progress. She expressed how she wanted us to concentrate on certain areas of her body and mind. We anointed her every time, and put her prayer shawl on while we prayed what Mike Evans called "soaking prayer."

God did a miracle in our friend Lois's life! Little by little, she improved. Now, she is her old self again.

Two years ago Lois was part of the leadership of American Baptist Women in our church. I rejoice to report that, last year, she joined our Wednesday night intercessory prayer group.

God used what we learned at Green Lake to make a difference in Lois's life. We were blessed to have her join us at the 2018 conference.

Leadership and administration have changed in our church over the last twenty-five years. We have learned to adapt and go with the flow. Many of our original conference attendees have been called into other ministries, fellowships, and church plants. City-wide prayer ministries have emerged from those beginning years in the First Baptist prayer groups. Our calling to pray in our church is still the same, but we do it within the parameters of how our leaders want us to serve in the Prayer Ministry.

I often feel reminded to look back at that first word Gary Clark and Joe Atkinson gave for our church: *We are not to get ahead of the Holy Spirit, nor are we to walk behind the Spirit. Rather, we are to walk so close to the Holy Spirit that we are in step with him, walking along side of what he is doing.*

5

THE HOLY SPIRIT AND HEARING GOD
REV. DR. LEE B. SPITZER

A PLACE TO HEAR GOD

On June 30, 2010, the Holy Spirit unexpectedly spoke to me about my future in an unprecedented manner, through a person I barely knew. Years later, I am still pondering and experiencing the fruit of that encounter with the Holy Spirit.

Located in central Wisconsin, Green Lake Conference Center has served American Baptists and other organizations for almost seventy years. I have enjoyed attending retreats, conferences and denominational meetings there throughout the years and in all four seasons. It is a sacred space for me, a place where I like to listen and talk with God and center my soul. On my daytime prayer walks, I might climb up the Judson Tower and take inspiration from beautiful views of the lake and surrounding property.

It has been my perennial practice to walk through the grounds late at night, after most others have retired to their rooms, and quietly consider my relationship with God and his will for my life. As I walk down quiet roads and paths, carefully wind my way along the shoreline, or slowly stroll through Memory Lane and the Vesper Circle, God has often spoken to my heart.

A PROPHECY AT GREEN LAKE

Holy Spirit Renewal Ministries hosts an annual conference at Green Lake, and in 2010 I was invited to teach on how the Holy Spirit guides our spiritual journeys and friendships. Following my sessions, I decided to sit in on a subsequent plenary session. Wanting to be able to use my laptop, I headed towards an empty chair in the back of the conference hall, next to Hannah Ford.

Hannah Ford D'Alessandro is the daughter of Cheri and Clay Ford, national co-director of Holy Spirit Renewal Ministries. They had introduced me to Hannah at the beginning of the weeklong conference. A singer and songwriter, Hannah had assisted in leading some of the worship sessions. At that time, Hannah was not yet married.

As the session progressed, we struck up a friendship, commenting on what we observed and laughing at witty comments. The next day I sat alongside Hannah once again, and after some time passed, she turned serious and asked if she could show me a drawing she had felt led to create. She interpreted it as a message for me from the Holy Spirit.

On the unlined back of a Green Lake notepad page, Hannah had re-created the four circle diagram I use to illustrate the varying intensities of relationships people experience. "Team L&L" and a heart dominated the center bullseye, a clear acknowledgement that for decades, my wife, Lois, has been my closest friend and ministry helper. Four lightning bolts pierced the four circles and continued outward, accompanied by the phrases "huge impact" and "increasing influence." Two sentences, one on top, and the other at the bottom of the drawing, stated: "You will draw people in to learn more and more. Your core circle will be a... power house sending God's heart and light and truth affecting all your circles and beyond." On a personal note, Hannah added, "I am one who was impacted."

This small paper is a gift I have cherished, and I confess that I have never received anything like it before or since. A dynamic drawing of my future life and its journeys, to my soul it resembles prophecy more than sweet sentimentality or appreciation. Through the years, I have reflected on its meaning, in light of the changing circumstances of my spiritual and vocational life. Three of the lightning bolts are similar, and to me refer to growth in my ministerial influence and impact as a pastor, teacher and historian/author. The fourth bolt, I sense on an intuitive level, may refer to changing priorities in how my wife and I hope to invest in God's kingdom work as we enter the "retirement years" of our lives. Specifically, we seek to empower innovative church ministries and future generations of ministerial and academic leaders.

Perhaps in another ten years, I may revise the interpretation in light of new surprises and experiences. What will not change is my conviction that the Holy Spirit spoke through Hannah and the drawing she created. Her artwork and thoughts have encouraged me to remain faithful to my calling.

THE SPIRIT SPEAKS THROUGH MANY MEANS

Throughout our lives, the Holy Spirit provides guidance for our spiritual journeys in a startling variety of ways. The modality God may choose is not significant in and of itself. One way is not necessarily more spiritual or special, but rather is based on God's assessment of how to best communicate with us at specific times in order to reveal wisdom and insight regarding our spiritual journeys.

Throughout the Scriptures, we see that the Spirit may speak directly to our souls, through words, impressions, feelings or intuition. God spoke directly to and held conversations with Adam and Eve in the Garden of Eden (Genesis 3:8-19). God spoke with Abraham to reaffirm the covenant and promise him a child in his very advanced age (Genesis 17:1-22), and with Moses on several occasions, including his call to serve as Israel's ambassador to Pharaoh (Exodus 3:1-4:17) and later, on Mount Sinai, when Israel received the Law (Exodus 19-20). At the end of his life, God spoke one last time to this great spiritual leader, in a poignantly intimate conversation on Mount Nebo (Deuteronomy 34:1-4). The Torah concludes with this amazing epitaph, "no prophet has risen in Israel like Moses, whom the LORD knew face to face" (Deuteronomy 34:10).

Nevertheless, God kept speaking to Israel's political leaders, priests, and prophets, so that they could fulfill their divine commission. The Scriptures understate the extraordinary nature of this form of divine guidance by often simply declaring, "the LORD said to..." (see, for example, Joshua 1:1). In the prophetic literature, an analogous phrase is often employed: "the word of the LORD came to me" (see Ezekiel 27:1 and 28:1; Joel 1:1; Micah 1:1, to cite just a few examples). We, as modern readers, are not given any clue regarding how these people recognized it was God speaking to them, or exactly how the message was conveyed. Did God converse in an audible voice that others who may have been present could have heard? Or, as is most likely, were the messages usually conveyed through the "gentle whisper" that Elijah heard, when God's voice was made manifest within his soul (1 Kings 19:12-18)?

In addition to spoken words, in the Old Testament the Spirit spoke through Scripture reading, circumstances, dreams, and visions. Dreams played a major role in Joseph's spiritual journeys. When he was just seventeen years old, Joseph's dream predicted his pre-eminence over his siblings. Understandably, they were not enthusiastic about what God had purportedly revealed (Genesis 37:1-11)! In Egypt, he was empowered to decipher the predictive dreams of others, including Pharaoh (Genesis 40-41). Centuries later, Daniel would leverage the same spiritual gift while in the service of Nebuchadnezzar (Daniel 4). Since the capacity to dream is a common human ability, regardless of spiritual condition, the Scriptures present occasions when those "outside the faith" receive dreams with a divine origin; see, for example, Abimelech (Genesis 20:3), and Pilate's wife (Matthew 27:19).

Throughout the Bible, dreams prove to be versatile in their ability to convey God's will. Gideon receives assurance that he will be victorious over the Midianites by surreptitiously listening to the sharing of a dream between enemy soldiers (Judges 7:9-15). Solomon asks God for the wisdom he will need to rule over Israel through a dream (I Kings 3:5-15). In the Gospels, Joseph was repeatedly guided by dreams. Through this medium, he was encouraged to stay committed to Mary (Matthew 1:20). And following Jesus' birth, dreams guided Joseph as he and his family went into exile and back (Matthew 2:12-22).

Similarly, visions communicated God's will to people throughout the Scriptures. In the cases of Ezekiel (Ezekiel 1, etc.), Paul (2 Corinthians 12:1-10), and John (the book of Revelation), Holy Spirit-inspired visions contained significant spiritual and theological discoveries. Daniel's epic conversational encounter with God, in which he sees the four kingdoms of human history, is initially described as a dream, but later on it is described as "a vision at night" (Daniel 7:1-13). Note that Paul's famous Macedonian vision takes place "during the night," and thus may have been a dream (Acts 16:9-10). Since in Hebrew poetry, lines reiterate similar ideas, Joel's Pentecostal prophecy confirms the close relationship between dreams and visions: "your old men will dream dreams, your young men will see visions" (Joel 2:28; Acts 2:17).

Although in general it may be said that dreams occur while one is asleep and visions happen while one is awake, the real point is that both modalities of divine communication function in basically the same manner. Through both dreams and visions, God speaks to us via the pathway of the mind's (or soul's) unconscious realm, in a manner analogous to how a television received signals in the era when they utilized antennas to receive broadcasts, or in today's world, through the internet. Whether you watch a show live or recorded, it is still the same show. In the same way, it really does not matter whether a dream or vision carries God's message. What counts is that we receive and act on the message God has shared.

THE SPIRIT SPEAKS THROUGH PEOPLE

The Holy Spirit utilizes diverse modalities to communicate with God's people, but not all of them necessarily include ecstatic or mystical dimensions. In fact, such revelations are rare throughout the course of our lives, and tend to be manifested at critical junctures of our journeys. Perhaps the most common method God chooses to communicate guidance and wisdom is possible to experience on any day - if we are willing to open up our heart, mind and soul to another person who knows how to listen to God and who cares for and loves us. This is the pathway of *spiritual direction*, comprised of two or more people listening and speaking to one another, and together seeking God's voice. Such a person may be a close friend, a mentor or teacher, and every once in a while, even a stranger whom God causes to cross our path.

There are numerous biblical stories of one person receiving insight into God's will or spiritual truth by listening and sharing with a wise and caring relative, friend or mentor (who is often, but not necessarily older and more spiritually mature). Abraham receives God's blessing through Melchizedek (Genesis 14:18-20; see also Hebrews 7:1-4). Moses' deep and devoted relationship with his father-in-law, Jethro, was an ongoing source of wisdom for the leader of the Israelites during the Exodus (Exodus 4:18; 18:1-27). Samuel, in his youth, received mentoring and guidance from Eli, during a period when "there were not many visions" (I Samuel 3:1-19). Ruth's willingness to take advice and counsel from her mother-in-law, Naomi, had a profound effect on the course of Israel's political future (the birth of David) and salvation history (the birth of Jesus). Nicodemus sought out the teacher from Nazareth under evening cover to fulfill his thirst for spiritual insight (John 3). Ananias risked his life by ministering to the newly converted Saul of Tarsus. His prophetic words not only commissioned the former persecutor of the church, but revealed his key recurring journey themes (Acts 9:9-19). In his early years as a Christian leader, Paul relied on the wisdom and encouragement of Barnabas as they served God together (Acts 9:26-27; 11:22-30; 13:1-3).

If God has so many means by which the Holy Spirit may communicate assurance, wisdom and spiritual direction, why does God also speak, as it were, indirectly through other people? I would suggest three reasons.

First, *discerning God's will and the attainment of spiritual wisdom is best achieved in consultation with others,* especially if they are more mature and experienced.

In a most fundamental way, this is illustrated by the intergenerational imperative of Deuteronomy 6:6-7: "These commandments that I give you today are to be on your hearts. Impress them on your children. Talk about them when you sit at home and when you walk along the road, when you lie down and when you get up." Similarly, the journey toward wisdom and adult spirituality is framed as a conversation between parents and children: "Listen, my son, to your father's instruction and do not forsake your mother's teaching" (Proverbs 1:8). The sharing of wisdom across the generations, the guidance of mentors and teachers, and the assistance of friends who support our journeys, are evidences of the Holy Spirit's participation in our lives.

Second, God's propensity to speak through people is *an affirmation of the relational nature of the Kingdom of God*. Growth in Christian spirituality and doctrine is more than just a solitary cognitive or intellectual achievement; it involves a deep appreciation for the impact our journeys have on others, as well as our dependence on the experience of others regarding our own faithfulness. The various gifts of the Holy Spirit are exercised in large part within the community of faith. We employ them to edify and strengthen the body of Christ (1 Corinthians 12:12-31). Similarly, the fruit of the Spirit require the presence of others to be actualized (Galatians 5:22-26). How can one grow in love, peace and joy in isolation from other people?

Third, being open to the possibility that the Holy Spirit may speak to us through other people *encourages the growth of humility and accountability* in our souls. Although applicable to all disciples, this insight is especially important for the spiritual health of leaders in the body of Christ. As we deepen our prayer lives and become more proficient in hearing the Spirit's voice, we become open to the seductive allure of pride (Proverbs 16:18). The antidote to this temptation is to keep one's soul open to the advice and counsel of others. Such accountability cultivates humility, which creates possibilities for God to bless our journeys: "plans fail for lack of counsel, but with many advisors they succeed" (Proverbs 15:22). Stated more positively, "listen to advice and accept discipline, and at the end you will be counted among the wise" (Proverbs 19:20).

HEALTHY RELATIONSHIPS, FAITHFUL JOURNEYS

Listening to the counsel of trustworthy teachers, mentors and friends promotes healthy relationships within the body of Christ and facilitates the faithful living out of our spiritual journeys. Such dependency is not a sign of weakness, but rather an affirmation that we are a part of a spiritual community and movement of God that is much larger than any individual. This does not diminish the significance of our individuality, but rather places it in its proper context.

For individual disciples, listening to others serves as an invaluable spiritual discipline. During key moments of our lives, it is always helpful to receive affirmation or warnings concerning the decisions that impact our future. Discussion with others provides the Spirit with opportunities to clarify situations, deal with our doubts, and make us aware of unseen possibilities or potential problems.

For spiritual leaders, the voices of trusted advisors and companions often reflect the Spirit's intention to protect us from over-inflated estimates of our own importance and wisdom. If our understanding of a situation reflects God's perspective, or our eagerness to lead a congregation or ministry in a specific direction accurately encompasses God's will, it should be able to withstand the sympathetic and sometimes critical reactions of others, who seek to support our journeys.

Throughout my life, I have deeply appreciated the input of others, through whom I have sensed the leading of the Holy Spirit. This can happen in many different ways. As an author, I have adopted the practice of accepting 90% of the changes suggested by my editors. This reminds me each time that my writing is improved by the insights of others, making them a gift from the Spirit. As a pastor and spiritual leader, listening to the perspective of other leaders and co-workers provides balanced understandings of the challenges before us, as well as protection from mistakes we might make. Accordingly, for example, I prefer to confer with my closest friends and colleagues before making any major vocational transition. I trust the Holy Spirit to speak through these special journey companions.

And every once in a while, don't be surprised if a person unexpectedly enters your life and hands you a creative drawing, or some other gift, which touches your soul and encourages your heart. The Spirit enjoys such surprises!

Hannah's Prophetic Drawing

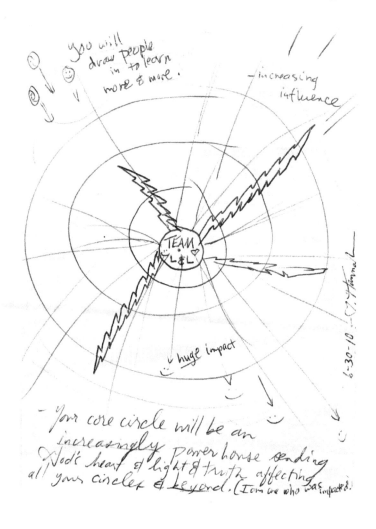

you will draw people in to learn more & more.

—increasing influence

TEAM L&L

6-30-10 :: Hannah

huge impact

— Your core circle will be an increasingly power house sending God's heart & light & truth affecting all your circles & beyond. (I am one who was impacted.)

54

6

THE HOLY SPIRIT AND FAMILY
NORELLE LUTKE

"I'm going to Green Lake without you!" declared our fourteen-year-old son. We were momentarily speechless. This was a quandary every Christian parent would love to have, a young teen insisting on going to a Christian conference, with or without you.

Attending the Holy Spirit Renewal Ministries Conference had become a spiritual high point in our kids' lives. We had been going regularly from the time they were little. This conference had become a place to have a fresh encounter with the Lord. It was a time and place for an infusion of biblical truth and Holy Spirit empowerment. It was a time and place to challenge teenage mediocrity and compromise, and to experience God. It was a time and place where it was acceptable to get on your knees and pray, to shed tears of repentance, to pray for others unabashedly, and see God move in miraculous ways. It was a time and place to see the Green Lake family from distant places, *and* to have lots of fun! Our son's question was, "How could we *not* be going to Green Lake?"

At the moment of his declaration I flashed back to a few years earlier. We had presented our children with the choice of Disneyworld, or Green Lake. We were astonished, and thrilled, when they chose Green Lake. Here we were with our young teen, happy that he wanted more of Jesus in his life, yet unsure of what to do. He solved the problem for us. In his determination to get to the Holy Spirit Conference, in a time before online access to information, he finagled a way to get there. We *only* had to drive him six hours each way to catch a ride with a "conference family." They were happy to have him tag along for the week. How could we say no?

We had become regulars at the conference, and loved it. Being there was a deep drink of cold water, from a well of living water, on a hot, parched summer day. We were drawn to this over and over again. This generational desire to be there went further back than us. It started with my parents.

My parents, Rev. Norman and Elva Blosat, were pastoring in Kingston, New York. During the Easter Sunday service of 1972 there was a visitation of the Holy Spirit that forever changed their lives, and the spiritual life of First Baptist Church of Kingston. In what had become a rigid, inflexible order of service, the Lord intervened and shook things up. There were interruptions, confessions, and testimonies of miraculous salvation. There was spontaneity under the inspiration of the Spirit that was prophetic in nature. Pastor Norm himself had a personal experience of seeing a shekinah glory cloud descend upon the church body. First Baptist experienced a sovereign act of God that day. They were never the same again.

Soon after this we discovered there was a great move of God happening all over the world. It was the early 1970s, and revival was happening across denominational lines wherever hearts were hungry for more of God. During this time, called the Jesus Movement and the Charismatic Movement, Catholics and Protestants were experiencing the fullness of the Spirit. They were discovering a spiritual inheritance for them that was untapped and unrealized. It was the kind of empowerment the early New Testament church had known.

Christians were discovering a personal Pentecost. The gifts of the Spirit had not died with the apostles, but were manifestations of the Holy Spirit for the church today. Healing was for today! Deliverance from demonic oppression was for today! Faith to do the greater works Jesus promised was for today! People were discovering that the truths of scripture about these and other provisions were not quaint theological points of interest from long ago and far away. They were alive, pulsating, practical out-workings of the Holy Spirit.

There were American Baptists of the ABC-USA denomination who were hungry for more of God. God responded to them during this worldwide revival. Ours was not the only American Baptist church experiencing sovereign workings of the Holy Spirit. At a biennial convention of the ABC-USA my parents were thrilled to discover pastors who had equally amazing testimonies of the Lord interrupting their ecclesiastical comfort zones.

It was a thrill to find others of like-experience and like-mindedness. This became a tremendous source of encouragement to all of them. Out of this emerged a loose-knit fellowship of Spirit-renewed and empowered ABC brothers and sisters, which quickly became a support and spiritual lifeline. A fellowship was born, which today is known as HSRM.

The continued felt need for mutual uplifting led to the planning of an annual gathering at the Green Lake Conference Center. Thus began the Holy Spirit Renewal Conferences. Those founding participants came back year after year to be part of this move of God. As of today, four generations have been impacted in eternal ways by what God does at the gathering. The power of this fellowship is the presence of God among us, hearts that continue to seek him, and the love of the saints that flows deep.

My family story illustrates the life-impacting effect of attending the Holy Spirit Conference, and why HSRM continues in its mission of holding conferences and special events throughout the year. The overarching organizational ministry objective is to help churches, individuals, and generations of Christians go deep in the Lord, know that God has a destiny for them, and have authentic, biblically strong, Spirit-filled experiences with the Lord, in settings where people learn to live lives of seeking him.

This objective has been accomplished as HSRM's leaders have stayed teachable, willing to learn from other streams of the Body of Christ outside of their own movement. No one group has it all, and there is much to learn from others.

An attitude of not living from fear, and trusting the Holy Spirit for discernment, has allowed for great spiritual depth, breadth, and empowerment in the HSRM movement. Instead of becoming ingrown, legalistic, and protective, conference attendees have been stretched, enlarged theologically and experientially, and empowered by hearing from a variety of godly leaders and teachers.

HSRM's leaders have been fearless, not only because they have learned to discern error by the Holy Spirit's anointing and guidance, but also because they know and search the Word of God. Being Baptists (also sometimes referred to as "People of the Book"), the Bible is held forth as the objective standard of truth by which to test teachings. A great distinctive of HSRM is the balance of Spirit-filled experience and biblical accuracy. What a great deposit to carry over to the next generations!

BIBLICAL PRECEDENT FOR SPECIAL SPIRITUAL EVENTS

Someone might ask if it is necessary to host conferences and special events? Aren't we encouraging people to chase after experiences and mountain-top spiritual highs? Shouldn't it be enough to just stay in my Bible? Isn't attending my own church sufficient? In response, as we look to God's Word we quickly see in the biblical narrative that God often called together large gatherings of his people, for the sake of conferencing with them.

For example, in Exodus 19, at the base of Mt. Sinai, God wanted his people to have a doubt-shattering encounter with him. He desired to deliver instructions that would shape them morally and serve to protect them. He wanted to establish a powerful identity in them.

Through Moses, the Lord called the people together. Experiencing his presence in this large gathering was significant for the children of Israel. They had audible proof of God, with heavenly trumpet sounds, God's own voice, and corporate visual evidence of his presence. This was accompanied by manifestations of smoke, descending fire, and shaking ground. Not only were God's instructions made abundantly clear, but God's heart for his people and their destiny was revealed to them.

Exodus 19:4-6a says,

> *You yourselves have seen what I did to Egypt,*
> *and how I carried you on eagles' wings and brought you to myself.*
> *Now if you obey me fully and keep my covenant,*
> *then out of all nations you will be my treasured possession.*
> *Although the whole earth is mine,*
> *you will be for me a kingdom of priests and a holy nation.*

What a God-encounter! Their God-designed destiny was declared. This was not a destiny they decided for themselves, or assumed from what others had told them. God identified who they were, for themselves, and for the rest of the world. This is the beauty of gathering together to hear from God today. God can use special gathering times to reveal his character, to express his desires for us, to instruct us, and to clarify our identity and destiny.

In Nehemiah chapters eight and nine we see another gathering of God's people to hear from him. This particular conference led to a national revival.

After being exiled in Babylon for seventy years, Ezra the priest read the Book of the Law to the Jews who had returned to their homeland. The hearing of the Law caused the people to shed tears of sorrow for how far they had fallen from God's standard. They acquired a new understanding of things that were holy to the Lord. They were strengthened by the joy of the Lord as God made it clear how to get things right. They feasted, repented, reestablished God's standards as prescribed in the book, and separated themselves from the sinful behaviors of the surrounding people groups. They covenanted with the Lord to live holy lives. This resulted from the collective, special-event encounter they had with God and his Word.

Jesus had special gatherings to accomplish different purposes. I like to think of conferences, special meetings, and retreats as gatherings where together we hear important messages from him. One example is the Sermon on the Mount. With thousands around him, Jesus delivered major truths revealing the "greater than" message of the Kingdom of God, which is far greater than the law. Arguably, the Sermon on the Mount is the most influential speech ever given. Here was direct revelation from Immanuel, "God with us." Here was an invitation to life with a heart pure toward God and in relationship with him. What a departure from the law-focused living the Jews were immersed in. This was a paradigm-shifting event!

Jesus had a habit of gathering followers together in small groups to reveal major truths and Kingdom messages that were not revealed to all people at the time. For example, in Matthew 17 Jesus takes Peter, James, and John to the Mount of Transfiguration. That was a mountain top experience of the mind-boggling kind!

Then there was Matthew 24, as Jesus spoke in detail about the consummation of the age and his second coming. Imagine if some of the disciples had decided to skip going up the Mount of Olives with him. If they had let common worldly cares keep them away they would have missed this important message from Jesus.

Those Jesus-conferences must have been awesome for his intimate circle of followers. They were times to remove themselves from the demands of daily ministry, rest in the comfort of his presence, and receive special mentoring as Jesus opened the mysteries of the Kingdom to them.

My experience is that Jesus-conferences haven't changed. Taking ourselves out of the ever-present distractions of normal daily living, purposely dedicating that time to hear from him and rest in his special attention, is a way to get awakened out of spiritual complacency and routine-induced dullness. Jesus is eager to answer our heart cries and draw us into his inner circle to hear revelatory, life-changing words. The Word of God remains true. "He [still] satisfies the thirsty and fills the hungry with good things." (Ps. 107:9)

The Holy Spirit Renewal Conference is a Jesus conference where we hear from God. Jesus said, in John 16:12-15:

> *I have much more to say to you, more than you can now bear.*
> *But when he, the Spirit of truth, comes, he will guide you into all the truth.*
> *He will not speak on his own;*
> *he will speak only what he hears, and he will tell you what is yet to come.*
> *He will glorify me because it is from me that he will receive*
> *what he will make known to you.*
> *All that belongs to the Father is mine.*
> *That is why I said the Spirit will receive from me what he will make known to you.*

All age groups need encounters with God. We are told to "train up a child in the way he should go so that when he is old he will not depart from it." (Proverbs 22:6). Yes, this admonition speaks to parents. But there are many layers to training up children. The body of Christ plays a vital role as well. HSRM has become a strategic supplemental resource for parents in this training-up journey. Generations of families have found that bringing their children to the conference is a Godsend. Kids get away from their everyday routine and go where being "on fire for God" with other youth is not only acceptable but sought after. This becomes a tremendous tool in God's hand for spiritual breakthrough in their lives.

Getting kids to a place where they can have a personal experience with God is important. Parents and grandparents, aunts and uncles, friends and youth workers need to do whatever it takes to help them have a vibrant relationship with the Lord. Compromising or carnal Christians have little chance of faith survival, so a potent faith that looks like the Book of Acts is what we need to press into. That means going counter to our secular, post-Christian culture, and being diligent to stay intimate with God. In this way young Christian people can rise up, in love and power, in a secular environment.

If it isn't important to do everything within our power to pass on the life of God to every generation, why would the Lord have instructed his people to teach children all that is spiritually available to them? And to do this, using all possible means of instruction? Some of God's instructional strategies included strict observation of laws, multiple feasts and holidays (especially think Passover), memorial stones and altars, verbal memorization, and so on. Deuteronomy 6:5-8 is clear about the never-let-up mindset we need to adopt as his people.

> [5] Love the LORD your God with all your heart and with all your soul and with all your strength. [6] These commandments that I give you today are to be on your hearts. [7] Impress them on your children. Talk about them when you sit at home and when you walk along the road, when you lie down and when you get up. [8] Tie them as symbols on your hands and bind them on your foreheads.

HSRM has a mandate to pass on the Kingdom-deposit God has given us. A life of revival is what Jesus desires for all, from generation to generation. We don't need to wait for another visitation of God to walk in the "now" power and presence of God. But we do need to keep it alive in ourselves, and pass it on to others.

Young people need to see God moving in might and power. They need exposure to others who can teach them and demonstrate the things of the Kingdom of God, learning by what is caught, as well as taught. When they are exposed to the joy and satisfaction of living a naturally supernatural Christian life fueled by the Spirit's power, their faith gets exciting. When they see and experience God at work, holy hunger gets stirred up.

When God's people have hearts that seek him and long to hear from him, he meets with them. It is God's heart to bless his children! We do not have to beg him to satisfy our longings and fill our hungry souls. God has already said he will do this. "He satisfies the thirsty and fills the hungry with good things." (Psalm 107:9) Be convinced of his love for you. Know that "Happy are people who are hungry and thirsty for righteousness, because they will be fed until they are full." (Matthew 5:6 CEB)

HSRM has impacted lives by affecting the spiritual growth and empowerment of individuals, thereby affecting the spiritual legacy they create and pass on to their families. I have seen this in five ways.

1) By opening the Word of God to them under the moving of the Holy Spirit.

2) By making teaching available from varied streams of the Body of Christ that is stretching, challenging, and paradigm-shifting.

3) By guiding them in their understanding of the Holy Spirit and the Spirit-empowered life that is available to all Christians (the supernatural life as normal).

4) By upholding the core value of growing in relationship with God, in his presence.

5) By helping individuals maintain and strengthen an existing godly legacy, and activating a new, godly legacy where there hasn't been one.

HSRM impacts generations by providing a vehicle for every generation to experience a life-altering encounter with God. By proactively, purposefully making provision for all ages, HSRM creates a platform for God to work, multigenerationally. Young people have their own experiences with God, and not just a set of adopted beliefs about God. This helps each generation "own" their faith, giving them their own "God stories," and catapulting them into carrying the legacy of God forward.

Thankfully, there are many beautiful Jesus-communities across the world. And thankfully my family experiences HSRM as one of them, being much more than just another event to attend. If what is happening in HSRM seems attractive to you, I invite you to consider joining with us at our next conference. Here are some steps to take to get in on the blessings.

1) Reading this book is a good beginning.

2) Mind your mindset. What are you believing or disbelieving? Ask the Lord to show you the value of attending the conference and *his* mind on the matter for you.

3) Don't be casual in your attitude. Do whatever it takes to get yourself and others to this amazing move of God. Don't listen to naysayers.

4) Let hope arise that great things will happen. God desires to bless you through the conference. Come expecting.

5) Press on to achieve your goal. Many obstacles from the enemy come to discourage and dissuade. Fight through in Jesus' name.

6) Don't miss the next one!

7

THE HOLY SPIRIT AND IDENTITY
PAM WANTZ

To put it simply, I didn't know what I didn't know.

I have loved God from the age of four. Much of what I learned about the Godhead over the years emphasized God as Father, God as Son, but not God as Holy Spirit. My understanding of the transforming role of the Holy Spirit was incomplete. It was as if I read the scriptures like this: "In the Name of the Father, the Son, and, oh yeah, the Holy Spirit." I did not realize it at the time, but in the late 1990s the Holy Spirit began to challenge my diminished theology. It happened like this.

I was holding on to unforgiveness towards my father. One afternoon, when I was alone, the Lord made it clear to me that not forgiving someone is a sin. Unforgiveness interferes with our relationship with God and distorts our perspective of our Heavenly Father.

I could no longer stuff my emotions about dad. I was done treading water spiritually! I needed support and accountability to walk through this decision. So, I called my sister, our knees hit the floor, and I confessed.

I asked for forgiveness for every offense, hurt, and lie which the Lord brought to my awareness. I sobbed throughout the process, but felt cleansed, reassured, and filled with his peace and love for me.

After this, within just a couple of months, my spiritual journey with Christ radically changed. I remember talking with my husband, Doug, about how I wanted to go deeper with the Lord. I was seeking something more. I was being personally challenged to keep growing as a believer.

Not long after I verbalized this desire the Lord put a schooling opportunity in my path. God said, "This is it!" He directed me to resources outside my normal circle of teachers. My eyes were opening to areas of scripture I had been overlooking.

Those years were some of the most exciting, challenging, and transforming of my spiritual life. The Holy Spirit was revealing himself to me. God was purging me of bad theology, and filling me with love for him and for people. Little did I know he was preparing me to be a pastor.

In 2009 a friend and fellow pastor told me about the Holy Spirit Renewal Conference. This was a yearly gathering at the end of June, in Wisconsin, at the Green Lake Conference Center. The Holy Spirit was opening another door for me to learn. I could not wait to go!

The week in Green Lake brought many new experiences with the Lord. The worship, the teaching, the beautiful property, and the precious people we met all made us feel like we were at the best family reunion ever. The teachings of the HSRM leaders, and the speakers over the years, have been key contributors to knowing who I am in Christ, and who he is in me.

The conference of 2013 was impacting to Doug and me in many ways. It all started the night before the event kicked off, as we had dinner in the cafeteria at the conference center. There we met and spoke with one of the guest speakers, Leif Hetland.

We listened to many amazing stories of Leif's ministry in the Middle East. This was a prelude to a week full of divine encounters. At every meal we ate in the cafeteria one of the speakers would end up dining with us. I asked the

Lord, "What is going on here?" We felt honored to have this personal time to hear further testimonies of what God was doing around the world, in the speakers' ministries. The Holy Spirit impressed upon my heart to just receive the many blessings he was pouring out on my husband and me this week.

That Saturday night meal in the cafeteria was the beginning of a power-filled week. The coming messages on intimacy, identity, power, and authority in Christ through the Holy Spirit changed me! I knew nothing about Leif Hetland, but after our first dinner together I was excited to hear more.

Leif has been called an "Ambassador of Love." He refers to the Father as "Papa God." I had heard God referred to as "Papa" before. But when Leif said it, something felt different. The intimacy of his relationship with God was so beautiful!

I felt God's loving presence every time we interacted with Leif, and while he was speaking. He taught us that, as God's children, we grow in our identity in Christ as we live our lives out of a position of rest in God. Power and authority come from knowing who we are in Christ.

Leif reminded us that many believers carry an "orphan spirit" (like someone who has lost their father), instead of living dependent on our Heavenly Father through his Holy Spirit. This orphan spirit flows against the many scriptural promises declaring we are adopted sons and daughters, heirs of the Most High God.

Leif gave a teaching using three chairs as a visual illustration for evaluating how we make decisions. As a believer, I am either choosing to rest in a holy, intimate relationship with Papa God (Chair One), or running around striving to figure out life on my own (Chair Two). Chair Three represents the person who does not know Jesus.

Staying in Chair One is dependent on an intimate relationship with Jesus, through the Holy Spirit.

In Matthew 11:29-30 Jesus tells us what life In Christ looks like. He says, "Simply join your life with mine. Learn my ways and you'll discover that I'm gentle, humble, easy to please. You will find refreshment and rest in me. For all that I require of you will be pleasant and easy to bear." (The Passion Translation)

In John 17, Jesus prays for those who are his disciples. He prays for our protection, and our unity as one body, just as he is one with the Father. Jesus prays for us to experience and enter in to the same joyous delight he and the Father have with one another, to overflowing. Jesus prays for our hearts to be guarded from evil, because we no longer belong to this world. He says, "Your Word is truth! So, make them holy by the truth."

He commissions us to represent him, as the Father commissioned Jesus to represent the Father. And then, Jesus dedicated himself to us as a holy sacrifice, so we would live fully consecrated to God, being made holy by his truth.

As I listened to God speaking through Leif, the same joyous delight Jesus experienced with the Father was again offered to me, and to all who love and follow him. The Father's love was re-presented in us! When the week was over, and Leif said good-bye, I cried tears of joy and gladness.

At another evening meeting Robby Dawkins demonstrated what power and authority look like when we know our identity in Christ. He gave personal testimony of his life and travels around the world. Robby shared how the Lord gives him words of knowledge about people, which open doors to share the gospel and pray for their healing.

As a demonstration, Robby asked if anyone in the room was experiencing back pain. Several people came forward. "Healing," said Robby, "is the work of the Holy Spirit."

He explained how much the Lord loves us and wants a personal relationship with each of us. What struck me most was how Robby prayed. He spoke simple prayers of authority over the first person, commanding parts of their back to be healed, and for pain to get out, in Jesus' name. Then, Robby checked with the person, as to whether the pain level had gone down, or left completely.

Once Robby finished praying for the first person (who, by the way, was healed), he directed *them* to turn and pray for the next person, and so forth. Every person in the group who had back pain received a healing. Every person healed received an impartation of God's love, which they promptly passed on to the next person. This is how the kingdom of God works, and it is so simple!

In Luke 9:1-2 we read: "Jesus called the twelve apostles together and gave them power and authority over all demons and the ability to heal sicknesses. He sent the apostles out to tell about God's kingdom and to heal the sick." (NCV) Through Robby, God was demonstrating what this can look like.

Robby drew upon what we read in Luke 10:17-20.

> *When the seventy missionaries returned to Jesus, they were ecstatic with joy, telling him,*
> *"Lord, even the demons obeyed us when we commanded them in your name!" Jesus*
> *replied, "While you were ministering, I watched Satan topple until he fell suddenly from*
> *heaven like lightning to the ground. Now you understand that I have imparted to you all*
> *my authority to trample over his kingdom. You will trample upon every demon before*
> *you and overcome every power Satan possesses. Absolutely nothing will be able to harm*
> *you as you walk in this authority. However, your real source of joy isn't merely that*
> *these spirits submit to your authority, but that your names are written in the journals of*
> *heaven and that you belong to God's kingdom. This is the true source of your authority."*
> (The Passion Translation)

When we returned from Green Lake I began to share what I learned and experienced with my congregation, Linden Avenue Baptist Church in Dayton, Ohio. I gave my testimony of what God had revealed to me. I shared how I saw God bring spiritual breakthroughs for many who grabbed hold of Leif Hetland's teaching on the orphan spirit. I illustrated this by using the three chairs. My flock could tell my heart was overflowing!

For the Sundays that followed God was showing what his truths look like for someone who rests in him by sitting in Chair One. As I demonstrated this by sitting in Chair Two, my people were being set free from lives of compromise, fear, doubt, and more. Chair Three was used to describe the person who lived a life without Christ.

The Lord showed us how similar chairs Two and Three looked. Some of our people reasoned it was more tormenting to live a life of compromise than to not know Christ at all. People were strengthened by this teaching. It encouraged them to spend more time with the Lord. Praise God that I had the privilege of witnessing believers and unbelievers being transformed from being spiritual orphans into God's kids, into the true sons and daughters of the Most High that they are!

On one of our Sunday mornings I took a risk, a step of faith, to demonstrate the Holy Spirit's power and authority by praying for people the way Robby did at the conference. Seven people came forward for healing. Before I prayed, I shared how much the Lord loves them, and desires intimate relationship with them. I then prayed for the first person's back, commanding parts of her back to come into alignment, and for pain to get out. After two times of praying, her pain was gone - she was healed! I then instructed her to pray for the next person, and so on. By the time we got to the last person, they were already healed. What a celebration of God's power in us and his authority working through us!

I love watching people get healed. As I reflected on what I learned through this conference, the Lord was highlighting and reminding me of my own journey of freedom in my relationship with him. Even though I had accepted Jesus' forgiveness, I had not given the same forgiveness to my earthly father.

Before the Lord revealed my heart to me, I was still a captive, sitting in Chair Two in a jail cell, with the door wide open. Until I forgave, and experienced deliverance from lies and past wounds with my earthly dad, my identity in Christ and my perception of Father God stayed messed up. Sadly, this is not uncommon in the body of Christ. I find many in churches who are experiencing an identity crisis as to who they are and who they are engaged to.

Today, I know I am the Bride of Christ, and that the Holy Spirit is making me ready for the wedding of the Lamb! The message of how to live victorious, empowered lives comes back to an intimate relationship with the Holy Spirit. I am learning to rest in him, by practicing being still before him. Jesus has shown me that when I surrender, he will always win the battle in me, through me, and for me. He is faithful, and just, and has transformed my thinking.

Now, when facing unhealthy stuff that threatens to diminish my joy in the Lord, I picture Jesus holding a trash can out to me. He points at my stuff: people, finances, fears, doubts, or complaints (it all stinks), and tells me to put these in the trash basket, right now. The Holy Spirit shows me lies I have been embracing. He reveals how they have influenced my thinking, and how they are *not* part of who I am in Christ.

As soon as I believe him, I flush the lie away, and experience him giving me power and authority to help others dispose of the same garbage. The Word of God *is* living and powerful! Jesus *is* the way, the truth and the life! He *is* the source of all knowledge and wisdom within each of us who believe!

Living in Chair One has shown me that confidence in Christ, in all things, is where I want to be seated as a believer. There are days I find myself slipping back into Chair Two, but not for long. Staying in the peace and rest of Chair One is a daily priority for my life. As Jesus says in Luke 11:36, "If your spirit burns with light, fully illuminated with no trace of darkness, you will be a shining lamp, reflecting rays of truth by the way you live." (TPT)

I know now that the Holy Spirit's transforming power and authority lives in me. I look forward to opportunities to share with others about Jesus, and how he has changed my life. I love to pray privately or publicly, for healing of any kind, and for deliverance. I love serving my Lord, who has seated me in the Chair of the Heavenly Places. And one day, I expect to carry the same anointing of love from Papa God that Leif Hetland experiences.

8

THE HOLY SPIRIT AND
BALANCED BOLDNESS
JOHN GROVE

I've been the pastor at Columbus Baptist Church in Columbus, New Jersey, for thirty-plus years. I was raised as the son of an American Baptist pastor. When I was seventeen, I had a life-changing experience. One night, alone in my bedroom, I heard God's voice for the first time. I wasn't praying; I was worrying. God reminded me of what the scriptures said about my situation. He guided me to make some big decisions and take bold actions the next day.

God did a miracle for me that day. The next evening, I felt his presence move into my heart (John 14:23), and he has been there ever since.

A year later, when I entered college in 1972, I got involved in house prayer meetings. In those meetings I became aware of the wonderful blessings of the "charismatic movement." I grew in knowledge and enthusiasm for God through the joyful worship and miraculous spiritual gifts at work.

Four years later I started pastoral studies at a solid theological seminary. While there, I received the precious gifts of Reformed theology, and gained proficiency in the biblical languages. Though my seminary held the official position that the charismatic gifts had ceased after the time of the apostles, I've never found that position to be intellectually or theologically tenable.

And besides, I was already experiencing what they said didn't exist! It was with this background of belief in the spiritual gifts, as well as a commitment to biblical authority, that I received the call in 1981 to serve my church, where I've continued to serve ever since.

Over the years I've tried to be careful to preach and lead in a way that is faithful to two towering truths: 1) the primacy of the written Word of God; and 2) the life-giving power of the Holy Spirit. I've seen many churches and ministries that, it seems to me, do not adhere to these two clear engines of spiritual health and growth. This leads either to spiritual weakness or weirdness. I keep this in mind whenever I consider allowing a guest to preach or teach at our church.

Eight years ago I received a phone call from Dr. Lee Spitzer, who was then the Executive Minister of the American Baptist Churches of New Jersey. Dr. Spitzer asked me if I'd like to have Dr. Clay Ford preach at our church on a Sunday coming up in three weeks. Clay was the director of Holy Spirit Renewal Ministries. This ministry has been in existence since the 1970s. It started out as a branch of the American Baptist Churches, USA. It is no longer officially affiliated with ABCUSA, but still retains many mutually beneficial interests and connections.

Being careful about who preaches at my church, I immediately wondered whether Clay would bring an inspiring and helpful message, or whether we'd be enduring a bunch of strange and crazy stories. When the topic is the Holy Spirit, you never know!

Since Clay came recommended by my trusted friend, Dr. Spitzer (now the General Secretary of ABCUSA), I thought it was worth the risk. Besides that, Lee suggested that I read Clay's book to get a clear idea of Clay's theology of the Holy Spirit. It is titled *Called to High Adventures: A Fresh Look at the Holy Spirit and the Spirit Filled Life*.

I was so pleased and reassured by what I read! It was an exciting work about how the Holy Spirit can and does work today, rooted in solid biblical truth. Now I was really looking forward to Clay's coming!

On the Sunday he preached, I was not disappointed. His message was powerful and sane. There was not a trace of hype, but rather biblical truth and powerful hope. Our people were so moved that many returned that evening to hear more, and to receive prayers for healing. Thus I observed a key distinctive of HSRM that I value so much – Balanced Boldness! That is, Biblical Primacy via Holy Spirit Power.

After that experience I was excited to learn more. I started attending HSRM's annual conferences in Green Lake, Wisconsin. I always return home with renewed confidence in boldly praying for healing, help, and miracles.

A THEOLOGY OF BALANCED BOLDNESS

The Spirit of God is a Spirit of bold power. (II Tim. 1:7) His Spirit equips us to believe boldly in Jesus's promises concerning prayer. Such as,

Ask and it will be given to you:
Seek and you will find.
Knock and the door will be opened to you.
For everyone who asks receives. . ...
If you . . ... know how to give good gifts to your children,
how much more will your Father in heaven
give good gifts
to those who ask him!
(Matt 7:7-11)

This passage, and numerous others like it, are a great encouragement to our faith. They stir boldness in our prayers, as well as our overall attitude toward our Christian life and witness. Over time, and with experience, we come to understand how our Spirit-filled lives can reflect the Balanced Boldness of God. One reason to expect miracles and healing is that it is modeled and taught as part of the promise for those in the Kingdom.

Two extremes are to be avoided, because they put us out of balance. On the one hand, we sometimes are timid and hesitant in prayer. We speak in spiritual generalizations. For example, "Oh Lord, please bless this sister and guide the doctors, so that if it be thy will, she might be healed." There's certainly nothing wrong with such requests. But have you noticed how much more direct, specific, and expectant are the prayers of Jesus and the apostles? "In the name of Jesus Christ of Nazareth, walk!" (Acts 3:6)

Though it is true that there was special authority vested in the prayers of Christ and the original apostles, nevertheless God clearly commands that those who believe should pray boldly, expecting observable results. (John 15:7; James 5:14,15) The works of the Spirit should be obvious enough to be recognized. (Galatians 3:2, 5; I Cor. 14:24, 25)

In the past five years, as I've heard testimonies and teachings at HSRM conferences, and searched the scriptures, I've begun to pray more specifically and expectantly. I usually see God respond to our expectant prayers with positive and exciting answers. Even when the result is little or no change, I continue to ask God for insight and grace to recognize his answers. Sometimes they eventually come in bigger and wiser results than I could have imagined at the time.

Frequently there is an immediate but partial healing. This doesn't discourage me; rather, I am encouraged to continue to pray, and see God's healing happen incrementally.

For example, I've seen the paralyzed eventually walk, and the blind eventually see, after years of praying. I've learned not to be afraid to pray boldly. Even if nothing seems to happen, the people feel blessed by God's love through prayer.

On the other hand, it is an erroneous extreme when people believe they have such a complete grasp of the mysteries of divine healing, prayer, and miracles, that they predict, even demand, that God *will* and *must* give the exact results we expect. In doing this we exceed the promises of God, which we're commanded not to do. (Rev. 22:18) Thus, if the person is not healed, we assume it is the fault of the petitioner, who must lack faith.

It is true that sometimes it may be a lack of faith. Or maybe God has something bigger and better on the way. (Eph. 3:20) In either case, the Spirit can bring growth in faith and wisdom as we wait for deliverance to come.

Any honest prayer veteran will admit to instances where prayers are delayed or "unanswered." We will never understand all the reasons why. Even the apostles were disappointed sometimes (II Cor. 12:8,9). I smiled when I heard a well-known contemporary faith healer once say, "I can't be conceited. I pray for healings for a living."

HSRM leadership seeks to teach and model Balanced Boldness. By this I mean prayer and ministry that demonstrate confidence that there will be observable, powerful results. At the same time, it is governed by a humble submission to the Bible, and to the sovereign and hidden will of God. This mitigates the fear of risking an "unanswered prayer."

PRACTICING BALANCED BOLDNESS

Here are some principles of Bold and Balanced prayer which I follow:

1) Be a clean vessel for God to use. Live in continual repentance and submission to God. Maintain a good conscience and pure heart. (Psalm 66:18)

2) Pray specifically and expectantly. Assume you will see the miracle happen, or begin to happen, immediately. If nothing seems to happen, pray again. If you are praying for someone else, encourage them to keep praying expectantly over the days ahead. Even though Jesus and his apostles hit "home runs" and achieved perfect healings instantly, we often must continue to keep praying to incrementally push back the powers of sickness and darkness. Be confident in the ultimate healing, whether in this life or the next. Remember that our ultimate confidence is in the Healer himself.

3) When praying for healing, follow the example of Jesus and the apostles by speaking right to the aliment. (Acts 3:6) If it is appropriate and with permission, touch that part of the body. It is never wrong to speak to God (instead of the ailment) and ask him to heal it. But remember that his power to heal has been also delegated to you and is available through you. (Eph. 3:20, 21) Therefore you can pray, "Cancer, in John's lungs, be gone in Jesus' name!"

4) Be at peace that God is Lord over the "how" and "when." His plan is always bigger and better than ours. Expect that the answer to faith-filled prayer *will* be good and powerful. Relax, and enjoy watching him "move the mountains" over the next few days, months, years, in ways you'd never imagine!

5) Sometimes it's appropriate to pray "if it be your will," or "not my will, but Yours be done." (Luke 22:42) It depends on the motive in our hearts. It's not appropriate if our heart is doubting God will answer our prayers, because that is not faith. On the other hand, it is appropriate if our motive is to surrender to God's plans for how and when our healing will come, and what it may look like.

CONCLUSION

Over the years I've seen people healed, and mountains moved, through bold, balanced prayer. I have personally seen the blind and paralyzed healed, tumors disappear, pain greatly or completely relieved, and more. I've also been disappointed when the Lord did not do just what I wanted him to do. Sometimes the healing comes after the earthly lifetime of the sick person or their intercessor. Not even death is too late for God. Just ask Lazarus, Mary, and Martha! (John 11:21-25)

We should never leave the treasures of bold, balanced prayer unopened. It is better to not receive something we ask God for than fail to receive something because we were too timid to ask!

9

PURSUE A DEEPER FILLING IN THE HOLY SPIRIT
CLAY FORD

Have you ever sensed a need to be filled with more of the Holy Spirit's power, presence, fruit, gifts, anointing, or boldness in your life? I remember one such time in my own life, many years ago.

I was between seminary semesters, and served as a summer missionary in Berkeley, California, for the American Baptist Home Missions Society. I was one of four summer missionaries assigned to The Telegraph Avenue Project.

Working out of a church basement near the UC campus, our services included a Runaway Center, a coffee house, and one free meal five days a week. I had charge of the coffee house. Although I was able to make an impact for Christ in some lives, my experiences left me spiritually and emotionally depleted. Prior to this, I had worked in youth and college-career ministry at a large evangelical church. Things went well there, and I didn't feel inadequate in that context.

Berkeley, however, was another story! That ministry didn't involve nice, middle-class Christian kids. It plunged me into a world of war-deserters, communists, the mentally ill, gang members from the Oakland ghetto, drug addicts, and more. True, I did have some incredible experiences, which I wrote about in my first book, *Berkeley Journal: Jesus and the Street-People*. But as I returned to seminary, I had the unsettling sense that I had barely scratched the surface of Berkeley's desperate needs. While I knew the Holy Spirit was in my life, I also knew I needed a lot more of him to minister to the depths of need and brokenness I had witnessed in Berkeley.

Prior to Berkeley, I had been fairly ignorant of the Spirit's power and gifts. Now I felt a growing interest and hunger for more of him. I read a book about the Holy Spirit's ministry that answered many of my questions. Subsequently, alone in my seminary apartment, I prayed something like this: *Lord, if this experience of a deeper filling with the Holy Spirit is of You, and if it will help me be more effective in witness and ministry, and if I won't cause division over it — I'd like to have it.*

God answered my prayer! The Holy Spirit gently came upon me like warm oil, starting with my head, and then moving down my spine. I opened my mouth and began to pray in word-syllables I did not understand. It felt like my spirit and God's Spirit were intertwining in some significant and powerful way.

Thereafter I noticed a deeper delight in worshiping the Lord, a greater boldness in preaching and sharing my faith, and a new expectancy and release in the operation of spiritual gifts.

That experience markedly changed my life and ministry. And, it left me with a life-long quest: I want *MORE* of the Holy Spirit!

Every believer should want more. After all, we need him for virtually every aspect of our Christian life and ministry. Consider these amazing things that the Holy Spirit does in us.

He gives us life.
He illuminates our intellects.
He sanctifies our emotions.
He refines our character.

He instills godly values and reverence for God's Word.

He motivates our wills and empowers our witness.

He moves our hearts.

He enables a relationship of love and trust with God.

He enables us to perceive the spiritual dimension of life and to navigate effectively in it.

He makes God's presence real to us and inspires our worship of him.

He fills us with love and makes us a family.

In short, the Holy Spirit makes the Christian life a great adventure! And that's why I cry over and over again: *COME, HOLY SPIRIT!!!* I know we already have him, but I know also that we need *more* of him! We need him to fill us to overflowing, not only as individuals, but as churches.

THE MANDATE TO BE FILLED WITH THE SPIRIT

The purpose of this chapter is to present to you several compelling reasons why you and I, and our churches and ministries, must be filled with the Holy Spirit. Paul urges us,

> *Look carefully then how you walk, not as unwise but as wise, making the best use of the time, because the days are evil. Therefore, do not be foolish, but understand what the will of the Lord is. And do not get drunk with wine, for that is debauchery, but be filled with the Spirit* (Ephesians 5:15-18, ESV).

Be filled with the Spirit.

The Greek New Testament verb for "be filled," *plēróō*, is in the imperative mood. That means it's not an optional suggestion, but an authoritative command. It's addressed to all the believers, not just one. The verb is in the passive voice, as in *let the Spirit fill you*. And, it is present tense, which connotes an ongoing filling, multiple fillings - continuously being filled by believing and appropriating what God has given us.

We pull out the rocks and the weeds in the garden of our souls, and we let *him* fill us. Paul is saying that we must allow the Holy Spirit to fill us, because we cannot possibly live this Christian life effectively and victoriously without him. The days are evil, and in order to make the most of every opportunity in these days, we *must* be filled with the Spirit!

When pondering what it means to be filled with the Spirit, I thought of how a natural-gas water heater works. Have you ever turned on a shower on a cold morning and waited for it to get hot, but it never gets hot? Somehow the pilot light has gone out. So, you turn off the water, and go relight the pilot light. Then, you wait an hour, and turn on the shower again. But it's still cold! Why? What did you fail to do? Wasn't lighting the pilot light enough?

When you accept Christ, it's like lighting the pilot light. Jesus said,

> *Unless one is born again, he cannot see the kingdom of God. . . unless one is born of water and the Spirit, he cannot enter the kingdom of God. That which is born of the flesh is flesh, and that which is born of the Spirit is spirit.* (John 3:3-6, NKJV).

You received Christ, the Holy Spirit gave birth to your human spirit, and you became a child of God. But does that mean you are filled with the Spirit? Returning to the water heater analogy, yes, the pilot light is lit. But the water is still cold! What do you have to do now to make it hot? You've got to go back to the water heater where you see a red knob that has different settings, MILD...MEDIUM...HOT. If you want hot water, you must turn the knob up to *HOT*. You'll hear the burning gas go *whoosh* as it moves throughout the base of the water heater and begins to heat the water. After a while, you get back in the shower, and *YES*, it's wonderfully hot!

Sisters and brothers, if you have accepted Christ, you've been born again, and the Holy Spirit dwells in you. However, if you want to make an impact ʼr God's Kingdom, that's simply not enough. To make a real difference Christ in this world, it will take far more than your human abilities, ingenuity, intellect, and eloquence. It will take the Person, presence, and power of the Holy Spirit working in and through you -- and in, among, and through our churches. That means we have got to turn the knob to HOT! We must earnestly pursue a deeper filling with the Holy Spirit!

COMPELLING REASONS TO PURSUE A DEEPER FILLING OF THE HOLY SPIRIT

There are many compelling reasons why we all need to pursue God for a deeper filling of the Holy Spirit. Let's look at several of these.

COMPELLING REASON #1: WE NEED TO PURSUE A DEEPER FILLING OF THE SPIRIT, BECAUSE WE NEED HIS POWER.

Paul writes in I Corinthians 4:20, *For the kingdom of God is not a matter of talk but of power* (NIV). So much of the Church today has reduced Christianity to propositional doctrines and creeds. Of course, we do need the truth of the Gospel. We need sound doctrine, because the Holy Spirit won't honor false teaching. Jesus is *the Truth* (John 14:6), and the Holy Spirit is the Spirit of *Truth* (John 14:17). But no matter how eloquent, well-researched, and conscientiously prepared it might be, teaching that lacks the power of the Holy Spirit is dismally inadequate. We may convince intellects, but have we moved hearts and wills? Have lives been changed, restored, and healed? Have captives been set free? How we need the Holy Spirit!

We learn from Acts 1:8 that we receive *power* when the Holy Spirit comes on us. The early Church, when first persecuted, prayed for boldness, and for the Spirit's power with accompanying signs and wonders. (See Acts 4:29ff). Their prayers were answered!

In Romans 15:18-19, Paul wrote that he had not fully preached the Gospel unless he had preached in *words* (doctrinal truths), through *deeds* (by his actions and lifestyle), and by the *power* of signs and wonders through the Holy Spirit. To him, these were all key elements of what it means to preach the Gospel. Why is it, then, that so often we are content with words and deeds, but omit the Holy Spirit's *power* – a demonstration, a manifestation, of the Kingdom of God?

Paul says the Kingdom is not about eating and drinking (Rom 14:17). It's not about religious rituals, or potlucks, coffee, and cookies. While these things can be meaningful and enjoyable, they are peripheral. The Kingdom is the presence and reign of God, through Christ, in the power of the Holy Spirit.

I find it difficult to understand why so many churches abdicate the realm of the supernatural, leaving it to cults and the occult, New Age gurus, and mediums. No doubt, many are skeptical of the supernatural because they've heard unbalanced teachings, or seen wild and crazy things done in the name of the Holy Spirit. Thus, some decide not to focus on the supernatural, or pursue it at all. But here's the problem with that. We live in a culture where most people *need* supernatural help for their problems. They need hope; they need healing, miracles, guidance, and direction. When the church offers them only intellectual teachings and superficial fellowship devoid of the life-changing and miracle-working power of God, they will go somewhere else. Why? Because they are *desperate!*

How ironic! Think about it. We have the God who created the heavens and earth with a word. We have the Savior who walked on water, healed every disease that he encountered, and cast out evil spirits with a word, a touch, or even a look. And, we have the Holy Spirit who has done, and is doing, signs and wonders all over the world. Our God has absolute *power* and *authority!*

Isn't it strange that so much of the Church is content not to have that power in a world that is increasingly experiencing the powers of darkness? We should be crying out to God like those early Christians in Acts 4:29-30.

> *Now, Lord, consider their threats and enable your servants to speak your word with great boldness. Stretch out your hand to heal and perform signs and wonders through the name of your holy servant Jesus.*

We pray every summer with that joyous boldness and expectancy at our Green Lake Holy Spirit Conferences, and at our other events around the country. And, by God's grace and to his glory, hundreds of people have been healed, restored, and delivered. Our God is an awesome God who loves people, and he can do anything!

Some Christians today say, *Well, God doesn't do those supernatural things anymore.* Says *who?* Why would anyone try to limit what the Holy Spirit can or will do, when we live in a world that needs his presence and power so desperately? We have only just begun to see Satan's evil manifestations in this world. Think about all the racial and ideological hatred and violence in our country. Think about the mass murders in schools and public places, drug addictions, sexual perversions, bondages, and suicides. And, because the devil knows his time is short, things will almost certainly get darker before the return of Christ. Listen: *The Church of Jesus Christ cannot afford to be powerless in a world that is increasingly experiencing the powers of darkness!* We *must* seek the Lord for an enormous outpouring of the Holy Spirit!

COMPELLING REASON #2: WE NEED TO PURSUE A DEEPER FILLING OF THE SPIRIT, BECAUSE THE HOLY SPIRIT GROWS OUR CONFIDENCE IN WHOSE WE ARE, AND WHO WE ARE, IN CHRIST.

Jesus tells us, in John 4:21-24, that the Father seeks worshipers who will worship him *in Spirit and in truth*. In other words, he seeks worshipers that are genuine, who know and love him personally. The Holy Spirit enables us to cry, *Abba, Father.* As Paul writes, *the Spirit himself testifies with our spirit that we are God's children* (Romans 8:15-16). Through the indwelling Spirit we can know God, not as an abstract concept, but as an amazingly wonderful Person.

I came to Christ during my senior year of college. It was around Christmas time when Jesus stepped out of the Bible and into my heart. I found out that God is real. I felt his enormous love, and wept on and off for days. Experiencing God's love for me changed my life forever. I had been a party guy, living a horribly reckless lifestyle, caring only about myself. But God loved me anyway. As he melted my heart, I wept over the realization that he loves everybody - people of every race and nationality and creed. God was no longer an abstract concept or theological syllogism. No, God is my Dad. He's my Father, and I feel his loving presence. In his great love, he has given me identity, meaning, and purpose. I love him, and have learned to trust him.

The Holy Spirit enables us to know *Whose* we are and *who* we are in Christ. He convinces us that we are sons and daughters of our Father in heaven. He is the One who empowers us to transcend the stifling expectations of other people. He enables us to rise above the dehumanizing experiences and the boxes and categories people try to shove us into. When we suffer debilitating wounds and rejections, he comforts and restores us. By his power we rise above the stereotypes and judgments other people try to put on us - the comparisons, jealousies, the traps of one-upmanship and never-matching-up that we often fall into. He reveals to us our true value and identity, as beloved children who are cherished and affirmed by our Heavenly Father.

Being filled with the Spirit makes it all real to us. He opens the eyes of our hearts to know not only our identity, but also our authority as believers in Christ. We have been made alive and raised up with Christ (Ephesians 2:4-5), and we are seated with Christ at the right hand of God in the heavenly places (spiritual dimension) - the place of favor, authority, power, and victory (Ephesians 2:6). What *joy* it brings us to see people at our Holy Spirit conferences become aware of these amazing truths and experience enormous breakthroughs in their lives.

COMPELLING REASON #3: WE MUST PURSUE A DEEPER FILLING OF THE HOLY SPIRIT BECAUSE WE NEED A GREATER EXPERIENCE OF GOD'S GLORIOUS PRESENCE AND ANOINTING IN OUR CORPORATE LIFE AND MINISTRY.

What is church without the presence of God – some kind of social club, or civic organization? Years ago I led a retreat for fifty college kids for a church in Stockton, California. At one point they turned down the lights, lit some candles, and shared their hearts. Suddenly the presence of Jesus came into the room. He was so real - almost as if he were physically among us, touching person after person. Many students burst into tears. They had never experienced the presence of Jesus in such a powerful way, and neither, at that time, had I.

I wrote earlier about my summer as a street missionary in Berkeley. At the end of the summer, I held a communion service in the church basement. All kinds of people came: A bad-conduct-discharged Marine on LSD; young black men from an Oakland ghetto, wearing sunglasses, acting cool; some were mentally ill. Many of the coffee house and meal regulars attended. Also, the publisher of a Berkeley radical newspaper came, along with at least one atheist intellectual. A nervous, scoffing spirit showed itself at the beginning, but that quickly dissipated. We had candlelight only, with people sitting around the wooden electric-cable spools for tables. Cochise, an African-American biker who had found Jesus in prison, helped me prepare and serve communion.

I had taped some music: *Hello darkness my old friend...* I played a song and then talked about life - lonely, sad, hard. I played *Jesus Met the Woman at the Well* by Peter, Paul, and Mary, and shared how Jesus met this woman and loved her when nobody else did. I played song after song. One song was, *People care about social injustice, they care about the bleeding crowd. How 'bout a needing friend. I need a friend.*

The Holy Spirit began to touch people, to the point that you could have heard a pin drop. I said, "Come up and take communion if God is touching your heart. Just give your life to Jesus." Amazingly, people began to come forward and kneel as they partook of the bread and the cup.

Crying broke out all over the room. These crazy, hardened street people were being deeply touched. The young blacks from Oakland pulled off their sunglasses and knelt down, weeping and marveling, "Wow, that's real, man, that's so real!" A mentally ill kid from New York City, who had threatened me with a razor blade he kept in his boot, came up sobbing and sobbing -- his life was transformed! The radical newspaper publisher was shaken, speechless, eyes moist with tears as he looked deeply into my eyes, gave me a big hug, and walked quietly away into the night. The atheist, nearly pulling out his hair, exclaimed, "I didn't know church could be like this. What is this? I've never experienced anything like this!" And what was *this* that he experienced? It was the presence of Jesus, made real by the Person and presence of the Holy Spirit. How we need to pursue him!!!

COMPELLING REASON #4: WE NEED TO PURSUE A DEEPER FILLING OF THE HOLY SPIRIT BECAUSE, AS CHRIST'S AMBASSADORS, WE RELY ON THE SPIRIT'S CREATIVITY AND ORCHESTRATION IN OUR EFFORTS TO REACH PEOPLE FOR CHRIST.

I once heard Jack Hayford describe a vision he had. He saw what looked like a pile of brown leaves. However, as he moved closer, he saw that they weren't leaves at all. They were bent and rusted keys.

How many of us have keys on our key rings, or in a drawer or jar, but we have no idea what they're for? We don't want to throw them away, because we might remember what they're for. Bent and rusted keys — what good are they, unless they are cleaned, identified, and put to use for their intended purpose?

People can be like bent and rusted keys. We're made with a purpose. But somewhere along the way, due to sin, brokenness, and life's hardships, people are damaged (bent and rusted), losing sight of their purpose in life. Like the Samaritan woman at the well whom Jesus met, we all need love, forgiveness, encouragement, meaning, and hope.

The Holy Spirit can orchestrate circumstances in ways we could never imagine. One day I was preaching at my church in northern California. For some reason, I felt led to veer off from my prepared notes to share an experience Cheri and I had with a Native American man at a McDonalds in Elko, Nevada. Cheri told him that Jesus loves him, and he began to share with us all the heartbreak, brokenness, and confusion he had endured as a Native American. We apologized for the many things our race had done to rob him of his culture and for the suffering caused by broken treaties, and so on. We prayed for him, and God touched him deeply. With tears coming down his cheeks, he asked, "How did you know what I needed to hear?" We said that we didn't, but that God did.

I told that story and then went on with my sermon. After the service a guy approached me whom I'd never seen before. He had long hair, and was dressed in military garb. He was homeless, and lived in the redwood trees. He held a blanket with something wrapped inside it. And, he was shaking.

I said, "Hi, nice to meet you."

He replied, "I'd like you to have this."

Nervously, I asked him, "What's in the blanket?"

He repeated, "I want you to have this."

As it turned out, it was his prized possession, a 1944 Marine Corps machete. He had polished and sharpened it, and it was beautiful. I responded, "I can't take this."

He said, "You have to."

I asked, "Why? Why would you want to give it to me?"

He said, "I was on my way this morning to kill two people with this machete, people who have been mocking me. Some members of your church invited me to come to church with them, and they wouldn't take no for an answer."

The Holy Spirit orchestrated that! He gave people in our church – people like *you* – boldness to say, "Come on to church!" Even though he looked different, with kind of a wild look in his eyes, they said, "Come on, come on, it won't hurt you to go to church."

And there he was, with his blanket-wrapped machete that he intended to use to kill two people. But instead he came to church.

It was a packed service, and I hadn't noticed him sitting out in the congregation. But the Holy Spirit knew he was there, and he led me to preach a different message than I had prepared, a message that bore right into this man's heart. Here is where the story gets even more amazing. I asked him, "Is there any other reason you want to give me your prized possession?"

He answered, still trembling with emotion, "My mother is a Native American, and I have never heard a white man say 'I am sorry' before in my life."

He gave me his prized possession and, needless to say, now it is one of mine.

By God's grace, and the Spirit's coordination of our efforts to reach people for Jesus, this man heard Good News that day, and I was privileged to lead him in prayer to receive Christ as his Savior and Lord. We need the Holy Spirit because he causes miracles like this to happen. He's creative. He reveals strategies. He is the Activator of all God's gifts and resources and blessings. He activates our prayers. He activates the power of the name of Jesus and the power of the blood of Jesus. He activates our spiritual armor and all the weapons we need to claim victory in spiritual battle. He heals, restores, and gives courage. And we need to pursue his fullness!

COMPELLING REASONS.... AND THE LIST GOES ON!

Well, I am out of space! I could go on and on with many more reasons, but we need to stop here. We truly do need to pursue a deeper filling of the Holy Spirit. As much as we may value and love the Holy Spirit, the impact that we are making in our culture is relatively small. We need to turn the knob up to HOT! I pray we will all do that.

I'm sure I speak for all the leaders of Holy Spirit Renewal Ministries. We invite you to join us in our efforts to bring a deeper Holy Spirit life and ministry to Christians, churches, our nation, and the world. Join us as we pursue an ever-deeper filling of the Holy Spirit so that Christ's church will shine like the city on a hill and the light to the nations he has called us to be.

CONTRIBUTORS

Annie Dieselberg is a missionary with International Ministries serving in Bangkok, Thailand since 1994. As the Founder and CEO of NightLight International, Annie has a passion to see the global church and community compelled by love to free, heal, and restore all who have been broken and wounded by sexual trafficking and exploitation.

Clayton Ford has been a pastor and renewal leader for more than four decades. He is the author of Called to High Adventure: A Fresh Look at the Holy Spirit and the Spirit-Filled Life. Clay is National Co-Director of HSRM.

John Grove is pastor of Columbus Baptist Church in Columbus, NJ. He is also active in prolife, racial reconciliation, and ABCNJ activities. John serves on HSRM's Executive Committee.

Ross Lieuallen is pastor of First Baptist Church of Billings, Montana. Ross serves as Vice-Chairman of HSRM.

Norelle Lutke is Assistant Director of HSRM and lives in Wichita, Kansas.

Teri Nyberg is a long time member of First Baptist Church in Sioux Falls, S. Dakota. Teri has been a part of the prayer ministry and has helped facilitate prayer events, retreats, and conferences at First Baptist and in the city of Sioux Falls. Teri is retiring from her position as a manager in Child Nutrition with the Sioux Falls school district. She has been employed with them for 31 years.

Ed Owens is retired after a long-term pastorate in Lansing, MI. His love for spiritual renewal has resulted in his work as a consultant for ABC-MI churches working with churches in pastoral transition and his role as chairman of Holy Spirit Renewal Ministries.

John Piippo is pastor of Redeemer Fellowship Church in Monroe, Michigan. He is the author of *Praying: Reflections on 40 Years of Solitary Conversations with God*, and *Leading the Presence-Driven Church*. John is National Co-Director of HSRM.

Lee B. Spitzer is the General Secretary of the American Baptist Churches USA. He also served as the Executive Minister of the ABC of New Jersey, and pastored churches in Rhode Island, New Jersey and Nebraska. Lee serves on HSRM's National Service Committee.

Janice Trigg is a licensed professional counselor, serves on HSRM's National Service Committee, and lives in Shawnee, Kansas.

Pam Wantz is pastor of Linden Avenue Baptist Church in Dayton, Ohio. Pam serves on HSRM's Executive Committee.

For information on HSRM's conferences, activities, and opportunities,
and to invite one of our leaders to your church,
visit our website at hsrm.org.

CPSIA information can be obtained
at www.ICGtesting.com
Printed in the USA
FSHW012207161120

9 781973 663980